YOUR MONEY
YOUR PURPO$E

Christopher Mediate/Mediate Financial Services
6674 Tippecanoe Rd., Suite 5 & 6
Canfield, OH 44406
www.mediatefinancial.com

Your Money Your Purpose/ Christopher Mediate
ISBN: 978-1-9640461-12

Chris Mediate is registered as an Investment Advisor Representative and is a licensed insurance agent in the states of Arizona, Iowa, Florida, Maryland, Michigan, Nevada, Ohio, Pennsylvania, and Texas. Mediate Financial Services is an independent financial services firm that helps individuals create retirement strategies using a variety of investment and insurance products to custom suit their needs and objectives.

Investment Advisory Services offered through Mediate Financial Investment Advisory Services, LLC, a State of Ohio Registered Investment Advisor. Any media logos and/or trademarks contained herein are the property of their respective owners and no endorsement by those owners of Chris Mediate or Mediate Financial Services is stated or implied.

The contents of this book are provided for informational purposes only and are not intended to serve as the basis for any financial decisions. Any tax, legal, or estate planning information is general in nature. Please remember that converting an employer plan account to a Roth IRA is a taxable event. Increased taxable income from the Roth IRA conversion may have several consequences. Be sure to consult with a qualified tax advisor before making any decisions regarding your IRA. It should not be construed as legal or tax advice. Always consult an attorney or tax professional regarding the applicability of this information to your unique situation.

Information presented is believed to be factual and up-to-date, but we do not guarantee its accuracy, and it should not be regarded as a complete analysis of the subjects discussed. All expressions of opinion are those of the author as of the date of publication and are subject to change. Content should not be construed as personalized investment advice nor should it be interpreted as an offer to buy or sell any securities mentioned. A financial advisor should be consulted before implementing any of the strategies presented.

Investing involves risk, including the potential loss of principal. No investment strategy can guarantee a profit or protect against loss in periods of declining values. Any references to protection benefits or guaranteed/lifetime income streams refer only to fixed insurance products, not securities or investment products. Insurance and annuity product guarantees are backed by the financial strength and claims-paying ability of the issuing insurance company. Mediate Financial Services is not affiliated with the U.S. government or any governmental agency.

Any names used in the examples in this book are hypothetical only and do not represent actual clients.

YOUR MONEY YOUR PURPO$E

A Retirement Planning Guide for Finding and Fulfilling Your Life's Work

CHRISTOPHER MEDIATE

CONTENTS

*For my wife, Leslie
and my sons Christopher and Carson —
my enduring motivation*

Adversity's Gift
Loss Can Lead to Growth

In an ocean of literature on retirement planning, shelves are stacked with volumes dissecting the mathematics of money, from diversification and asset allocation to optimizing social security and mastering retirement plan withdrawal strategies. These are undeniably important pieces of the financial puzzle, and as a dedicated financial advisor, I've guided many through these intricate processes. However, they merely scratch the surface of what true financial planning encompasses and only begin to touch on the reasons that compelled me to pen this book.

The essence of financial preparedness, a theme I impress upon my clients repeatedly, is the anticipation of life's unexpected twists and the cultivation of a plan that can weather any storm. The pivot to this principle is a personal one, born from an evening that reshaped my life's trajectory and, in turn, my approach to financial guidance.

The transformative date was June 21, 2013—a quint-essential first day of summer. I recall the serene atmosphere, the warm air perfumed with the promise of the season, as I sat on the patio, savoring the company of my wife, Leslie. She playfully suggested that I skip my usual basketball game to enjoy the evening's tranquility with her. As much as her offer tempted me, my commitment to my friends awaited—our casual basketball gatherings were a tradition, albeit with sporadic attendance during the summer months.

That night, what began as a routine game evolved into a pivotal life event. Despite having finished my games for the evening, and poised to head home, a shortfall in players on the court beckoned me back for one final match. It was a decision that, unbeknownst to me, would profoundly alter my life.

As the game unfolded, a fast break transformed into an accident—a defender's attempt to block my shot ended in an unintentional, severe blow to my head, specifically my right eye. What I initially perceived as swelling from the impact was, in fact, a blinding injury. The following morning led to an emergency surgery that, despite its success, imparted a sobering prognosis: the likelihood of regaining sight in my injured eye was slim.

The ensuing months were a relentless cycle of hope and disappointment—five different procedures aimed at salvaging my vision, each concluding in vain. Enduring retinal surgeries meant spending countless days facedown, immersed in a forced stillness that profoundly shifted my perspective on life's fragility and the things we take for granted.

Throughout this ordeal, one silver lining became abundantly clear: the structures I had in place for my business had afforded me a financial buffer that allowed me to focus on recovery without the looming stress of financial ruin. This epiphany was striking—how many people find themselves unprepared for such unforeseen crises?

My personal adversity underscored the myriad of unexpected events that can upend one's retirement—market crashes, economic downturns, health crises, or the loss of a loved one. This realization fueled my mission to share my insight and assist others in fortifying their lives against the unpredictable, not only to survive but to thrive.

Ultimately, the loss of sight in my right eye didn't just affect my vision—it redefined my perception of what matters most. The accident was a catalyst for a greater understanding: that we are not always in control and that sometimes we must yield to the ebb and flow of life and trust in the journey. It is a philosophy that permeates my work and my desire to guide others toward seeing the larger picture.

Now, as I navigate the world with one eye, the reflection in the mirror serves as a daily reminder of life's ephemeral nature and the importance of truly living. My goal, which this book is an extension of, is to empower you to achieve a secure and fulfilling life, regardless of financial capacity. While many advisors set monetary thresholds, my advocacy is for financial planning that is inclusive, understanding that value is not solely quantified by net worth.

In these pages lies a synthesis of professional expertise and personal growth—a blueprint for resilience that transcends the traditional scope of financial advisement. It is a testament to living a fulfilling life, an approach that champions the idea that, with the right perspective and planning, contentment and security are within reach, no matter what life throws your way.

This is the cornerstone of my message and the heart of this book: adversity can be an unlikely gift, offering insights that lead us to grow and prepare in ways we never anticipated. Through my journey and the strategies outlined here, I invite you to discover how financial planning can be the conduit to a rich and rewarding retirement, woven with the threads of preparedness, adaptability, and the courage to embrace life's every twist and turn.

CHAPTER ONE

A Wise Retirement

"The greatest wisdom is in simplicity. Love, respect, tolerance, sharing, gratitude, forgiveness. It's not complex or elaborate. The real knowledge is free. It's encoded in your DNA. All you need is within you. Great teachers have said that from the beginning of time." - Lao Tzu

After a long and successful career, Susan was finally able to retire. She had worked hard her entire life, and she was now looking forward to relaxing and enjoying the fruits of her labor.

At first, she thought that retirement would be wonderful. But after a few weeks, she soon realized something wasn't quite right. The days felt empty and hollow; no matter what she did or what new hobbies she tried, nothing seemed to make her feel fulfilled anymore. It almost felt like there was a hole in her life—an emptiness

*that couldn't be filled with just relaxation and leisure
activities.*

*One day, as she pondered this discontent that plagued
her daily living, it suddenly hit her! She knew precisely
why retirement felt so monotonous: it was because she
had no purpose in life anymore! All the years spent
raising a family, building her career, and dealing with
the everyday struggles of life had given meaning to
every single action taken. But without any overarching
mission or objective guiding her now, all the days started
blending into one endless void of greyness.*

*That's when Susan decided enough was enough. If
having some kind of purposeful activity was what it
took for happiness, then by golly, she'd find herself an
adventure! She decided to fulfill her lifelong dream of
hiking the Appalachian Trail. Instead of conquering
the entire trail in five months, she decided to take her
time and hike different sections of the trail over several
years. This way, she could enjoy the journey piece by
piece and savor each experience. Susan spent many days
planning and preparing for each section of the trail and
enjoyed this process. It filled her days with purpose, gave
her a sense of excitement, and was always something
to look forward to. As she hiked the 2,200-mile trail*

from Georgia to Maine, Susan encountered a variety of challenges and met new friends along the way. She said that retiring gave her the time and freedom to pursue her adventure, step out of her comfort zone, and take her time to experience the trail fully.

Aligning Your Financial Plan with Your Purpose

Ask a typical Wall Street broker about the key to a happy and dignified retirement, and chances are, the conversation will revolve around money.

But with thirty years as a financial advisor, assisting hundreds of families to prepare for and move into retirement, I've learned that a fulfilling and purposeful retirement requires more than just accumulating wealth. To truly make the most of your life's efforts, it's critical to craft a retirement plan that resonates with your personal goals and purpose.

After retiring as a corporate lawyer, Jim Johnson decided to follow his passion for fishing and moved to Florida. He spent his retirement years fishing every coast and eventually started his own fishing charter. Jim says that retiring has allowed him to live his dream and share his love of fishing with others.

One of the key aspects of a purpose-driven retirement plan is understanding and budgeting for the costs associated with your desired retirement journey. Whether your purpose involves hiking the Appalachian Trail, starting a fishing charter in Florida, or doing service work abroad, there will be financial costs that need to be taken into account.

By understanding the cost of your purpose, you can structure your retirement plan to provide the income and withdrawals from savings that you need, when you need them. This means taking a careful look at factors such as your Social Security benefits, investments, and other retirement assets and ensuring that they are structured to provide the income you need to support your purpose.

After retiring from her job as a social worker, Barbara Hastings decided to combine her passion for travel with her desire to give back. She began volunteering with an organization that coordinates service trips abroad and has since traveled to several countries to help build schools, homes, and medical clinics. Barbara says that retiring has given her the freedom to pursue her passions and make a difference in the world.

It's also important to remember that a purpose-driven retirement plan doesn't have to be a one-time event. It requires reassessing your goals and adapting when needed.

Your goals and financial situation can change over time, so it's essential to be flexible and willing to adjust your plan as necessary to ensure that your retirement stays on track.

Ultimately, a purpose-driven retirement plan is about creating the life you want to live and using your financial resources to support that purpose. By aligning your finances with your purpose, you can enjoy the freedom and fulfillment that comes with a truly meaningful and rewarding retirement.

Did you know that the oldest recipient of the Nobel Prize was Leonid Hurwicz, who received it at the ripe age of ninety? Or that Dorothy Davenhill Hirsch set a new record when she ventured to the North Pole at eighty-nine? These seniors are proof that age is no barrier to finding and pursuing your purpose.

A Purpose-Driven Holistic Approach to Financial Planning

Traditional financial planning often focuses on techniques like asset allocation, tax reduction strategies, and optimizing Social Security benefits. While these are important elements of financial planning, they are not designed to allow you to advance or achieve your purpose. These strategies are designed to help you build wealth and secure your financial future, but they do not take into account the unique goals, aspirations, and purposes that motivate you.

A purpose-driven approach to financial planning is different because it puts your purpose at the center of the planning process. This means taking a comprehensive look at your goals, dreams, and aspirations and creating a plan specifically designed to support them. This approach not only focuses on financial security but also on the life you want to live.

After retiring as a high school physics teacher, Bill Landis decided to follow his passion for music. He spent his retirement years performing in local bands and eventually formed his own group, playing concerts and festivals around the state. Bill credits his fulfilling retirement to turning his love of music into his purpose and not letting his age hold him back.

This means that instead of simply focusing on strategies like asset allocation and tax management, a purpose-driven approach to financial planning also takes into account factors like the costs associated with your desired retirement journey and creates a plan that is structured to provide the income and withdrawals you need to support your purpose. It also allows for a more flexible approach since it includes assessing your goals and adapting when needed.

In short, a purpose-driven approach to financial planning is more than just a set of technical investment strategies. It's a holistic approach that takes into account the unique desires, goals, and aspirations that motivate you and uses that information to create a plan that will allow you to live the life you want in retirement.

At ninety-two years old, Harriette Thompson set the record for being the oldest woman to complete a marathon. But she didn't stop there. Just two years later, at ninety-four, she broke her own record by becoming the oldest woman to complete a half-marathon! What's even more remarkable about Harriette is that she didn't start running until she was in her fifties and didn't participate in her first marathon until she was seventy-six.

Breaking Away from Traditional Financial Planning

Traditional financial planning often falls short when it comes to helping individuals achieve their unique goals and aspirations in retirement. Wall Street brokers and traditional financial advisors tend to take a one-size-fits-all approach, offering generic investment strategies without considering each client's specific needs and desires. This approach may work for some, but it fails to address retirees' diverse and unique aspirations. It ignores the use of savings to pursue a person's purpose, and it is not tailored to the individual's specific needs, goals, and desires.

It falls short of genuinely helping individuals because it often focuses primarily on maximizing returns and minimizing risk in a retiree's portfolio. While these are certainly important considerations, they do not take into account the retiree's purpose and how that purpose may impact their investment decisions.

For example, a retiree planning to sail around the world would need more liquid assets, as that endeavor would require more access to money.

But from the perspective of many Wall Street brokers and traditional financial advisors, it might make their life easier if they assume that everyone will pretty much have the same lifestyle in retirement.

If you doubt this, consider many rules of thumb prominent in financial literature.

Rule of Thumb 1: You will need 80 percent of your pre-retirement income to live on when you retire

One example is the common rule of thumb used in traditional retirement planning advice that says a person will need approximately 80 percent of their pre-retirement income to meet their retirement expenses.

This approach completely ignores the very different financial needs and planning for a couple who wants to buy a mountain cabin to spend their summers on the lake with their grandchildren compared to a person who wants to become a professional scuba diving instructor.

And it can easily lead to other problems as well. Investment planning for retirement is often driven by the need for a portfolio to generate a certain amount of income to meet anticipated expenses.

When an individual's expenses don't really fit some rule of thumb, the portfolio could end up being structured in a less efficient way or entirely wrong.

When Tom Drummer retired from his career as a corporate lawyer, he knew exactly what he wanted to do with his newfound free time: pursue his passion for fine wine. Instead of settling into a comfortable retirement, he chose to take a chance and chase his dream. He enrolled in sommelier school, and after completing his studies, he began offering his expertise as a speaker at wine taster events. Now, he spends his days doing what he loves, meeting new and interesting people, talking about delicious wines, and running a successful and enjoyable part-time business.

Rule of Thumb 2: Your portfolio should be diversified with 60 percent stocks and 40 percent bonds

Another commonly used rule of thumb in traditional financial planning is the "60/40 Portfolio split," which suggests that investors should allocate 60 percent of their investments in stocks and 40 percent in bonds. This is a traditional way to balance risk and return in a portfolio. However, this approach has been increasingly questioned in recent years. Some experts argue that this rule of thumb is no longer effective in keeping money safe, given the changes in the market. The idea of the 60/40 split came from the last century, which had different economic conditions, and thus, this rule of thumb may not have the same effectiveness.

While some "experts" recommend modifying it to a 50/50 or 70/30 split, even these modified splits still do not take into account the importance of considering one's purpose in retirement and how that purpose may impact investment decisions. In order to determine the investments, asset allocations, and liquidity best suited for you, consideration must be given to how you intend to use your money to pursue your purpose. That purpose will dictate the time horizon for the money, liquidity needs, income needs, and more. This will help create a portfolio tailored to your specific needs and goals rather than adhering to a one-size-fits-all rule of thumb that may not be best for providing a fulfilling retirement.

*After retiring from her job as a high school principal,
Cheryl Morris decided to pursue her love of music by
starting a community choir. Cheryl had always enjoyed
singing and saw the choir as a way to bring people
together and positively impact her community. The choir
quickly grew in popularity, and Cheryl found great joy
in conducting and leading rehearsals.*

Rule of Thumb 3: You should delay starting Social Security

Another frequently shared rule of thumb you will surely hear is that it's always better to delay the age when a person claims Social Security to get a larger monthly benefit. While there is no question that delaying Social Security can provide a good deal of security later in life, it may not always be the best strategy, especially if it interferes with the purpose you want to pursue.

Waiting to claim Social Security until age seventy might make sense for some retirees, as it will provide them with a larger monthly benefit that can help support their retirement goals. However, for others, the trade-off may not be worth it.

The best financial plan looks at all available options and uses the one that gives you the security you need with the least sacrifice in terms of your purpose. It is not always about maximizing a monthly Social Security check if it comes at the expense of your ability to live the life you want. A good plan should take into account both your financial and your retirement goals and find a way to align them. It's important to consider all of the options available and make a decision that aligns with both your financial needs and your purpose in retirement.

Don't Sacrifice Your Health

Financial milestones shouldn't solely drive the decision of when to retire. If your job is causing undue stress or physical discomfort, continuing to work to achieve greater financial security could be counterproductive, risking your most valuable asset—your health. The stress and strain from a demanding job can have far-reaching consequences on your physical and mental well-being, potentially leading to increased medical expenses and a diminished quality of life in retirement.

An essential aspect of retirement planning is accurately understanding the financial cost of your retirement lifestyle. This understanding involves a comprehensive look at how various pieces of your savings and income sources fit together to create a cohesive and efficient retirement plan. Knowing your true budget and how much money you can comfortably live on is vital. This clarity helps in making an informed decision about when to retire without unduly sacrificing your health for financial gains.

As you navigate through the complex process of retirement planning, remember that your health is an invaluable asset. Don't overlook the physical and mental costs of continuing in a stressful job. Focus on creating a retirement income plan that aligns with your health needs and lifestyle aspirations. It's about making informed decisions that balance financial security with the richness of life and well-being. After all, the ultimate goal of retirement planning is not just to ensure financial stability but to enable a fulfilling and healthy retirement life.

Crafting Your Unique Financial Plan

With the right plan, just about anything within reason can be accomplished, including finding and pursuing your purpose in retirement. This approach to planning strives to give you the freedom to live the life you want in retirement but also ensures that you are taking a responsible approach with the best chance of being financially secure.

By striking a balance between your purpose and practical considerations, you can have the confidence and peace of mind that you will have enough money to fund your purpose while ensuring a secure and stable financial future. With the right plan, you can achieve a fulfilling retirement and be free to pursue your passions, fulfill your purpose, and live the life you want.

Creating a financial plan that's as unique as you are involves several layers. It starts with deeply understanding your current financial situation and future aspirations. It's about asking the right questions: What does retirement look like for you? What are your fears and hopes? How do you envision your lifestyle? What are the non-negotiables in your life?

Then, it's about translating these insights into a financial strategy that is flexible, adaptable, and aligned with your vision. It might mean prioritizing certain investments over others, choosing specific types of accounts, or planning for particular life events. The key is ensuring that every aspect of your financial plan is designed with your unique needs and goals.

Just as a woman chooses boots that fit her perfectly in style, comfort, and purpose, your financial plan should be a perfect fit for your life. It should resonate with your aspirations, provide comfort in terms of financial security, and align seamlessly with your vision for the future. Remember, the best financial plan is not just about wealth accumulation; it's about crafting a plan that fits you perfectly, enabling you to live the life you've always imagined.

Now it's time to get started and write your story...

After retiring, [your name] decided to pursue
(his/her) love of...

CHAPTER TWO

Pursuing Your Passion with Confidence

"Believe in yourself and all that you are. Know that there is something inside you that is greater than any obstacle." - Christian D. Larson

Pursuing a meaningful retirement is an exciting prospect for many people. While it's important to identify what will bring true purpose and fulfillment, it's equally important to ensure that one has a financial plan that allows for the pursuit of these goals. People must be responsible when considering a retirement plan—no matter how fulfilling the goal may be. You can't risk finding yourself old and broke later in life, no matter how fulfilling the early part of your retirement. The price tag of running out of money while you are still alive is simply too high.

Financial planning for retirement can be a confusing and overwhelming process for many people. One of the biggest reasons is that there are so many unknowns. How can you predict future expenses, inflation, investment performance, medical expenses, or how long you might live?

With all of the unknowns, it is difficult to confidently spend savings on things that bring purpose and fulfillment during retirement.

John and Sarah had always dreamed of traveling the world once they retired. They had saved for years and invested wisely to make it happen, and they were excited to finally set sail.

But just as they were about to depart on their adventure, the stock market took a sharp turn for the worse. Their portfolio, which was heavily invested in stocks, took a significant hit, and they began to worry about their financial future.

Despite their concerns, John and Sarah decided to go on the trip anyway. But instead of enjoying themselves, they spent most of the time worrying about their investments and regretted spending the money on the trip. They were afraid that the market crash would severely impact their retirement savings and didn't feel comfortable enjoying the trip fully.

Uncertainty can make it hard to feel comfortable spending money on travel, hobbies, or other activities. People may be unsure about how to invest their savings and how much they can afford to spend, leaving them paralyzed and unable to make financial decisions confidently.

Retirement planning is a complex task that involves making trade-offs between what you want today and what you want in the future, and it also involves dealing with a lot of numbers and projections. All these can make the process of planning for retirement overwhelming for many individuals.

But it doesn't have to be this way. With the right information and understanding of some fundamental principles, people can make informed decisions and confidently spend their savings on the things that bring them purpose and fulfillment.

Later chapters will provide the details, but for now, these are some key principles to focus on:

Principle 1 - Keep It Simple

Keeping things simple when planning the financial part of retirement is essential for ensuring the plan is implemented and followed. A complex plan can be overwhelming and challenging to understand, making it less likely that you will take the necessary actions to achieve your financial goals.

John was getting closer to retirement. He went to a financial advisor for help, but instead of a simple, straightforward plan, he received a fifty-page document filled with investment jargon, charts, and graphs. The plan was so complex that John didn't even know where to start, and it eventually ended up collecting dust on his shelf.

Simplicity is especially important when working with a financial advisor because, while they may have more experience and knowledge of financial concepts, they are not the one who will live with the consequences of the plan. A complex plan can be easily misinterpreted or difficult to follow and execute over time.

By keeping the financial plan simple and easy to understand, it will be more likely that individuals like John will take the necessary steps to achieve their financial goals. In this way, a simple plan can be a powerful tool for financial success.

Principle 2 - Income Is the Key

If you are like most people, during your working years, you relied on paychecks from employment not only to pay your bills but also to enjoy your life.

Think back to any time when those paychecks were in doubt. Whether it was due to the prospect of pursuing a new job, potentially being laid off from the job you had, a disability, or any other reason, once those paychecks were in doubt, your life was likely turned upside down. You worried, couldn't sleep at night, and had difficulty enjoying life.

Retirement could mean thirty years without a paycheck. So you have to create your own. That is what your savings and investments are for.

To ensure a secure and comfortable retirement, you should aim for at least one consistent income stream to cover your essential living expenses. And because you want a fulfilling retirement, you should aim to have a second stream of income that will allow you to pursue hobbies, travel, or other activities that give your retirement purpose.

Investment decisions can be overwhelming, and there is a lot to consider. However, the key is to keep things simple and focus on how your investment and other financial decisions will impact your future income streams. By considering this, you can make informed decisions that will help ensure a financially stable and fulfilling retirement.

Principle 3 - Have a Written Retirement Income Plan

Warren Buffett, one of the world's most famous investors, once said, "an idiot with a plan can beat a genius without a plan." That's good advice regarding successful investing and enjoying a secure and purposeful retirement.

Your money and your retirement are too important to just let things happen without preparation. You need a financial plan that offers flexibility to weather changing conditions and reliability so you don't have to spend every day worrying about your future.

Considering the previously stated principles of keeping things simple as you focus on income, the type of plan you need is a straightforward and easy-to-understand document that addresses four fundamentals.

- When your retirement paychecks will start
- Exactly which part of your retirement assets they'll come from
- How they will potentially grow over time to keep pace with inflation
- And perhaps its most significant value—it tells you how long those paychecks are going to last

It's one simple two-to-three-page document that lays all of this out in a language you can easily understand. Without it, you are left with only guessing if you have the income you need to pursue a fulfilling retirement and, more importantly, if you'll have enough to pay your bills.

Principle 4 - Your Portfolio Is Not a Plan

The difference between merely investing in financial products and crafting a lucid retirement strategy is substantial. Many people fall into the trap of thinking that a collection of stocks, bonds, annuities, and other financial instruments is synonymous with retirement security. This perspective, unfortunately, often lacks a tailored objective and might not align with an individual's specific needs.

Retirement planning transcends the simple aggregation of investment assets. Although investing is undoubtedly a critical component of retirement savings, it represents just one facet of a much larger retirement readiness plan. A truly successful retirement strategy encompasses a comprehensive view of your future.

Principle 5 - The True Meaning of 'Return on Retirement'

In my journey as a financial advisor, I've gravitated towards a unique perspective on retirement planning, one that steps outside the typical financial focus. The term "Rate of Return" (RoR) is a fundamental concept in the investment realm. Traditionally, RoR refers to an investment's net gain or loss over a specified period. It's a key metric used to gauge the performance of your assets. However, it's essential to recognize that an impressive "Rate of Return" on your investments doesn't inherently guarantee a fulfilling retirement.

We must pivot our focus to a broader and arguably more significant RoR—the "Return on Your Retirement." This concept transcends financial gains to encompass your retirement's overall satisfaction and fulfillment. It's about measuring the success of your retirement, not just in monetary terms but in the joy and contentment it brings to your life.

Consider the following scenarios:

1. **Early Retirement vs. Additional Savings Years:** The dilemma of retiring early to savor freedom versus working a few more years to bolster savings is a classic example. This decision isn't just about the financial implications; it's about weighing the value of time against money.

2. **Social Security Benefits Timing:** Deciding whether to claim a smaller Social Security benefit early or delaying for a larger payout isn't purely a financial calculation. It's also about considering how this choice aligns with your lifestyle goals, health, and longevity expectations.

3. **Relocation Choices:** The decision to move closer to family versus staying in a familiar community filled with friends isn't just a financial consideration. It's about evaluating each option's emotional, social, and psychological returns.

In each of these situations, the impact extends well beyond the realm of finances. They touch on personal happiness, social connections, health, and overall life satisfaction.

In my approach to advising clients, I advocate for a holistic view of retirement planning. It balances financial readiness with emotional, physical, and social preparedness. The goal is to maximize the "Return on Your Retirement" by crafting a plan that harmonizes your financial security with your aspirations, health, and happiness.

A fulfilling retirement isn't solely defined by the size of your bank account or the performance of your investments. It's characterized by how well your retirement years align with your vision of happiness, fulfillment, and purpose. It's about ensuring that your retirement plan isn't just financially robust but also enriches your life meaningfully.

A robust retirement plan is a well-defined roadmap detailing the route to your retirement objectives. It should address critical questions: How much capital is necessary for a comfortable retirement? When is the ideal retirement age for you? Which income streams will sustain you in your post-working years? A prudent plan considers predictable expenses like healthcare, leisure, and lifestyle costs and prepares for life's unforeseen financial demands.

With a thoughtful retirement strategy, you can make enlightened choices about the financial tools that best serve your goals. It allows for a personalized investment approach rather than a one-size-fits-all method.

Moreover, a comprehensive plan protects against the array of risks that could erode your retirement funds, including inflation, market instability, and unexpected costs. By anticipating and mitigating these threats, you safeguard your income and secure your retirement trajectory.

In essence, the act of investing is not a retirement plan in itself. You must devise a strategic, all-encompassing plan incorporating every facet of your life to secure your retirement. This strategy not only guides your investment choices but also fortifies your financial future against the myriad of risks that lie ahead.

CHAPTER THREE

Why Smart People Make Dumb Retirement Mistakes

It is curious yet true that smart people are not always wise.

Intelligence does not necessarily guarantee successful financial outcomes. The real key to success often comes down to how a person utilizes the available resources. Some of the smartest people have made disastrous decisions when transitioning into retirement, not because they weren't smart enough but because of their behavior and focus on the wrong things.

Talented individuals who lose focus during retirement can find themselves engaging in financial folly, while those lacking formal education or knowledge might still secure lasting wealth if they are savvy enough regarding their behavior.

One of the most surprising lessons I learned by observing so many clients transition to retirement is how many intelligent people make dumb mistakes. Here are some common ones you need to avoid.

Putting the Cart Before the Horse

Imagine this scenario: you're searching for financial guidance, so you decide to seek the expertise of a professional advisor. To ensure a well-rounded view, you set up meetings with three different advisors, each with the goal of shedding light on:

- What you've been doing right in your financial strategy
- What might be amiss in your approach
- How you can enhance your financial future

Your first meeting is with Advisor One. Right after some preliminary questions, this advisor requests your financial statements. While you're anticipating some validation of your financial efforts, the advisor quickly zeroes in on the negatives, enthusiastically suggesting how things could have been better under her watch. She inundates you with charts and figures, underscoring her prowess in investment management. You leave the meeting feeling more disoriented than educated, questioning your past decisions with little recognition of what you did well.

Then comes Advisor Two. Like the first, this advisor eagerly delves into your financial details, quickly fixating on "problem" areas. The proposed solution? To invest all your assets into an annuity promising guaranteed returns, seemingly safeguarding you against market downturns. While the pitch is compelling, it's unnervingly singular—invest everything into this annuity and do it swiftly.

Such experiences are not uncommon. The emphasis is heavily on investment choices—often the advisor's own. They're quick to present a fix, urging immediate action. What's glaringly absent is an earnest effort to understand you: your ambitions, dreams, and plans. This oversight is significant because investments should be a vehicle for realizing your life goals, not the objective itself.

It's the classic case of the cart before the horse. Without a grasp of your individual aspirations, how can an advisor's recommendations truly be pertinent to you? Financial products and investments are merely instruments to facilitate your life goals. Their efficacy can only be judged within the context of your unique situation.

Now, let's consider Advisor Three, who adopts a distinctively different tact. This meeting is about you: understanding your unique objectives and aspirations before even discussing how to manage your finances. Your portfolio performance is secondary to whether it's calibrated to your life's ambitions. It's not about the rate of return in isolation; it's about tailoring a financial strategy to meet your specific life goals.

If you're pondering which route is preferable, I'd urge you to lean towards the methodology of Advisor Three. This preference is because of a comprehensive focus on many retirement variables where the primary interest was in you and your life priorities. Advisor Three devoted time to uncovering your vision for life and potential obstacles to achieving it. Informed investment advice can only follow such an understanding.

In my practice, the approach is methodical, involving several discussions. It's not about immediate answers but understanding what's needed and desired for your life journey and how to enable it. The initial meetings are about laying the groundwork for a tailored financial plan—the investment strategy is merely one component of this comprehensive plan, which is, ultimately, all about you.

The Right Level of Risk and Reward

Understanding the indissoluble link between risk and reward is often undervalued in investment strategy. Many believe they grasp this concept, yet it might be more nuanced than presumed. This principle is particularly crucial when a financial professional evaluates your portfolio in the context of your broader financial plan. Despite the financial media and some professionals potentially portraying this as a complex issue, it's quite straightforward. The initial step in this process is to determine your portfolio's risk level accurately. This can be done with specialized software or by consulting with an expert, like me. Pinpointing this risk is vital, as it informs the selection of an appropriate investment benchmark for your assets.

Measuring the actual risk in your investment portfolio is a critical component of your financial strategy. It establishes realistic expectations for the range of returns you might anticipate and the extent of potential losses you could face. This understanding enables you to align the degree of risk in your portfolio with your comfort level regarding risk. After aligning these aspects, you can identify your investment benchmark. A benchmark is crucial; it acts as a measure to evaluate the performance of your investments against a relevant standard. It's also essential that the level of risk you undertake corresponds with the needs of your financial plan for it to succeed. An imbalance—taking too much or too little risk—could derail your objectives. Thus, it's important not to prioritize investment performance over the foundational strategy of your plan.

In the absence of a clear financial plan, determining a target investment strategy becomes guesswork. Once a plan is established, your investment allocation can be tailored to support your specific financial goals. When considering hiring an investment manager, it's imperative to have a benchmark that reflects the necessities of your plan, not just your appetite for potential returns. This benchmark acts as a guide: not just a measure of success but as a way to ensure your investments are aligned with the plan's objectives. Chasing high returns without regard to this alignment introduces risks that may not be justified by your long-term financial needs. Therefore, the benchmark you choose should represent what's essential for your plan's success rather than an arbitrary chase for higher returns.

To illustrate benchmarks, if your strategy involves full market exposure, you might use the S&P 500 as a benchmark. For a balanced approach, perhaps a mix of 50 percent S&P 500 and 50 percent Aggregate Bond Index might serve as suitable benchmarks. Alternatively, 60 percent in the S&P 500 paired with 40 percent in the Aggregate Bond Index would reflect a balanced portfolio. To clarify, as an investor with a portfolio comprising 60 percent stocks and 40 percent bonds, you would use a corresponding 60/40 index as your performance gauge. And if your investment style leans towards growth, mirroring the risk and return profile of the S&P 500, then the S&P 500 itself becomes your benchmark, reflecting your acceptance of market risk in pursuit of growth.

The significance of this becomes clear when we apply a tangible example. Imagine you're at the zenith of your career, focusing on investment growth. When you evaluate your portfolio, you uncover your actual risk tolerance, which aligns predominantly with the stock market. You conduct what's known as a stress test on your investments to measure this risk more precisely. This test is designed to simulate how your portfolio would perform in both flourishing and declining markets. Through this assessment, you come to understand that the volatility of your investments closely mirrors that of the S&P 500 index. This realization is crucial; it confirms that the S&P 500 is a fitting benchmark for tracking the performance of your investments.

Now, consider you've enlisted a financial advisor to manage your investments. Picture a scenario where you're reviewing your financial statements during a meeting. You're examining the performance: Your portfolio has yielded a 7 percent return. But the critical question is, how does one evaluate the advisor's performance? If they're tasked solely with managing your investments without a broader financial plan, how do you determine if their service justifies the cost? Let's delve into this with a hypothetical dialogue in my office. You present your statement, proud of the 7 percent return. My response might be less enthusiastic—"I don't know if that's good." You're puzzled, "What do you mean? It's a decent return, isn't it?" And here lies the crux—I'm not disputing the quality of the return; rather, I'm questioning what benchmark you're measuring it against. With your risk profile aligned with the stock market, as identified earlier, the appropriate comparison would be against a stock market benchmark like the S&P 500. Only then can we discern the true efficacy of your investment performance in relation to the risk assumed.

What if, upon comparing your portfolio's 7 percent return to the benchmark's 10 percent? It's clear that a 7 percent gain isn't inherently inadequate, but juxtaposed with the S&P 500's 10 percent—assuming equal levels of risk—it suddenly loses its sheen. You're facing identical risks, yet your returns don't measure up. This discrepancy is a crucial aspect of assessing true risk versus return. It's time to re-evaluate what your financial plan necessitates in terms of risk and return and select a benchmark that aligns with those requirements. This critical step ensures your investment choices propel you toward successfully realizing your financial objectives.

Furthermore, if you've engaged a financial advisor whose performance doesn't surpass the relevant benchmark, it prompts a crucial conversation about the value you're receiving for their services. Keep in mind the essence of investing isn't merely in the pursuit of high returns but rather in securing the returns essential for realizing the goals of your retirement plan. It's imperative to compare your returns against your benchmarks—it's that significant.

Not Planning for Taxes

It's quite possible to be astute in the art of wealth accumulation—as seen with an individual who amasses $3 million through the stock market—yet lack a strategy for tax efficiency. Take, for example, the person who, brimming with self-assurance due to not needing the funds immediately, continuously postpones tax payments. The introduction of Secure Act 2.0 might seem like a blessing, allowing deferrals until age seventy-three. However, this approach can be flawed, creating what I term a "tax time bomb." It's a looming issue for those who defer taxes without a detailed income strategy that addresses both current and future tax obligations.

In my conversations with clients, a common theme emerges: a fundamental misunderstanding of taxation, especially regarding marginal tax rates. It's an area that many avoid and only a handful, typically professionals, are willing to navigate. Nonetheless, understanding taxes is crucial in relation to your financial plan.

It's evident that clearly articulated goals are more than just a roadmap to your desired lifestyle and retirement; they are also your blueprint for legacy. By now, you may have recognized the importance of these written goals not just for the sake of your own future but also in the context of estate planning—ensuring that, should anything happen to you, your assets are distributed according to your wishes.

After thoughtful consideration, you might find your generous nature leads you to support charitable causes, preferring to allocate a portion of your wealth to philanthropy rather than solely to tax obligations. Such a realization can shape your estate planning priorities. You've determined a hierarchy for your legacy: family first, charitable causes second, and, as a last resort, the government. This hierarchy isn't just about who benefits; it reflects your values and the impact you wish to make with your accumulated wealth.

Understanding the significance of this is crucial because it empowers you to tailor your income strategy with tax efficiency and charitable giving at the forefront. While I'll delve into the specifics in the tax planning section, it's vital for you to grasp that you hold the reins when it comes to your finances. Resist the default path where the government dictates the utilization of your diligently accumulated savings. By proactive planning, you ensure that your money serves the purposes you value most.

Don't Lend Money to Family

Lending money to family or friends is often driven by emotion, a gesture rooted in compassion, and it's a choice that can be deeply satisfying. However, I advise my clients to have a conversation with me before they extend a loan. My intention isn't to dissuade them; rather, I aim to help them view it through the right lens—it's akin to giving a gift rather than making an investment. The reality is that the return of this money is far from guaranteed. Money, after all, is a renewable resource, so if you're comfortable with not getting it back, that's fine. Yet, I've witnessed such generosity strain, even sever, familial ties. If maintaining harmonious family relationships is integral to your life's joy, think twice before lending money. Ensure that your bond can withstand the potential loss because when money is lent under the guise of investment, it often becomes a gift inadvertently.

Underestimating Life Expectancy

The idea of "front-loading" retirement by aggressively spending money in the first ten years is a common sentiment that many entertain, but it's a strategy not without its pitfalls. Assuming that our later years will be less active might seem reasonable, but this is a risky gamble. Underestimating our longevity or potential for an energetic life in our 80s can lead to one of the more significant miscalculations in retirement planning. It's true. I've encountered numerous individuals in their 80s who exhibit remarkable vitality, often surpassing the younger generation in their zest for life. Therefore, depleting your resources early on under the assumption of a sloweddown future could jeopardize your financial security later on when you might still be very much capable of—and interested in—enjoying life's adventures.

Financial plans typically aim to preserve your assets until the age of ninety-five. This isn't to say that reaching ninety-five is a certainty, but it's unwise to dismiss the possibility. Consider the average life expectancies: eighty-seven years for women and eighty-four for men. If retirement begins at sixty-five, that potentially translates to a retirement period spanning two decades or more. Take a moment to reflect on your family history and health tendencies—these factors are crucial for a realistic retirement strategy.

It's vital to contemplate a future where your lifestyle remains vibrant into your later years. Skimping on this part of the plan isn't prudent; often, it's a mere justification for early overspending. Instead, it's advisable to err on the side of caution and plan for longevity. A life of leisure and activity well into advanced age isn't just a hopeful scenario—it's a very real possibility that your financial strategy should acknowledge and embrace.

Ignoring Health Care Expenses

The resolve to avoid a nursing home is shared by many—it's an entirely understandable sentiment. However, the reality is starkly different: nearly 70 percent of retirees will require some form of additional care during their later years. Steering clear of a nursing home doesn't negate the need for planning around future healthcare needs.

Whether it's in-home care or an assisted living arrangement, your financial strategy needs to incorporate a proactive approach to this potentiality. Ignoring it is not a viable option. It's essential to have a documented strategy in place that addresses this aspect of eldercare. Your financial plan should include a clear directive or set of actions that acknowledge and prepare for health-related expenditures that often come with advancing age.

Addressing the potential need for long-term care is essential to any comprehensive financial plan. The question is not just whether you can afford to self-insure or purchase insurance but how these choices align with your overall financial strategy and life stage.

If you opt for self-insurance, does your investment strategy still allow for growth, acknowledging that the need for capital may continue well into the future? If considering insurance, does your financial plan afford you the flexibility to cover premiums? You might evaluate whether to pay for a traditional long-term care insurance policy monthly or to leverage an asset for asset-based long-term care coverage. The decision to insure or not is significant, requiring a careful analysis of your current and future financial capabilities.

Furthermore, your plan must contemplate whether trust planning to protect and potentially distribute your assets is viable. It's imperative to consult with a knowledgeable attorney who can swiftly implement crisis planning, if necessary, to protect your estate from the potential drain of long-term care costs.

These are not mere details but pivotal decisions that shape the security and efficacy of your healthcare planning, directly impacting your financial well-being in later life.

Navigating the complexities of asset protection and long-term care funding can be fraught with misconceptions and simplistic solutions. A common piece of advice that retirees may come across is the idea of transferring all assets to children or placing everything into a trust to shield wealth from government reach. However, this is a misinterpretation of how these processes work.

It's not the government that directly claims your assets for long-term care costs but rather the care facilities. These facilities charge for their services until an individual's assets are depleted. At that point, when personal funds are exhausted, assistance programs like Medicaid may come into play to cover ongoing care costs.

What are the pitfalls of this mindset? Here's my perspective. You've toiled and saved diligently for your retirement, looking forward to this milestone that many of us aspire to. After such effort and planning, it seems counterintuitive to relinquish all your accumulated assets. The premise that you can transfer your wealth yet continue to enjoy unfettered access to it and maintain your current lifestyle is fraught with risk. The assertion that your children will manage the trust and ensure your financial stability without fail is overly optimistic. By adopting this approach, aren't you resigning yourself to potential financial insecurity? To reach retirement only to divest yourself of your resources seems akin to surrendering the very independence you've worked so hard to achieve.

The rationale behind such decisions warrants close examination. Initially, one must consider the location of these accounts in terms of their tax status. For tax-deferred accounts like IRAs or 401(k)s, withdrawals are taxed at your current ordinary income rate, potentially pushing you into a higher tax bracket and magnifying the financial impact. Furthermore, the IRS defines a gift as a transaction devoid of any expectation of reciprocal benefit, something that's genuinely at arm's length. If you retain access to the income from these assets, it might not constitute an arm's length transaction. I'm not in a position to offer tax advice, but this scenario certainly raises red flags. If you're contemplating this route, engaging with a knowledgeable attorney and tax advisor is essential. In my professional observation, it calls for an in-depth discussion and meticulous planning to ascertain the right course of action.

If purchasing insurance appears prudent due to concerns about future care, it's wise to consider it. For those with ample assets who prefer to self-insure, it's crucial to have a detailed long-term care strategy. This should explicitly outline from which assets funds should be drawn, your preferred type of care, and its desired location. A well-articulated plan can significantly reduce potential stress for your family. However, recognizing your situation and having a contingency plan ready is essential if neither insurance nor self-insurance is viable. This emergency strategy should be documented to guide your family through difficult decisions and alleviate undue stress. It underscores the importance of incorporating such preparations into your broader financial plan, aiming to mitigate the emotional and logistical load on your loved ones.

Overlooking the Creation and Updating of Legal Documents

In the realm of financial planning, the creation and maintenance of legal documents is frequently underestimated. As a financial advisor, one of the first tasks I undertake with new clients is ensuring that their estate planning documents are not only present but also up-to-date. This step is often the most neglected, yet it is essential for a comprehensive financial plan.

The core of estate planning begins with the will. Ask yourself: Do I have a will, and when was it last updated? It's more common than you might think for individuals to either lack a will entirely or to have one that's outdated. The same scrutiny applies to both financial and medical powers of attorney (POAs). When were these documents last reviewed? In the event of incapacity, these POAs are your voice, allowing others to manage your finances and health decisions according to your wishes.

Consider the significance of the financial power of attorney. In the U.S., saving for retirement often involves company-sponsored plans like 401(k)s and 403(b)s, which are appealing due to their tax advantages and potential for employer matching. Yet, these accounts are individually owned. What happens if the owner becomes incapacitated? Without a financial POA, even a spouse has no immediate access to these funds, which could be critical in managing household finances and medical expenses.

Medical POAs are similarly crucial and yet commonly overlooked. No one wants to leave their family with the burden of guessing their medical preferences during an emergency. A medical POA ensures that your healthcare directives are followed, representing your decisions when you can't make them yourself.

Wills are just one component of estate planning, and they often do not have the reach that many assume. Assets like IRAs, 401(k)s, and life insurance policies pass directly to the beneficiaries designated in those accounts, bypassing the will entirely. This means these designations must be actively managed and reviewed—ideally, on an annual basis—to ensure they align with your current wishes.

To circumvent the probate process for individual assets, such as bank accounts, consider establishing Transfer on Death (TOD) or Payable on Death (POD) designations. This simple step can streamline the inheritance process for your beneficiaries, sparing them the complexities and delays of probate court.

Regarding trusts, which can be either revocable or irrevocable, the choice depends on your specific needs and intentions for your assets. Revocable trusts offer flexibility and control, allowing you to alter the terms as needed, while irrevocable trusts can provide asset protection by placing assets out of your personal ownership.

Trusts articulate your wishes in detail, guiding how and when heirs receive their inheritance. They can be particularly valuable in complex family situations or when businesses or multiple properties are involved. They also afford privacy and expedite the transfer of assets since they typically bypass the probate process.

Trusts are not just for the wealthy; they serve a practical purpose for those concerned about the welfare of minor children or dependents with special needs, ensuring that the estate is utilized to provide for their long-term care and well-being according to your instructions.

Proper attention to the creation and updating of legal documents is integral to the success of your financial plan. This process safeguards your assets and ensures that your legacy is distributed as you intend, ultimately providing peace of mind and security for you and your loved ones.

The Importance of Fiduciary Financial Advice

When seeking financial advice, it's crucial to consult someone bound by fiduciary duty. But what makes this term so noteworthy in today's financial advice landscape? A fiduciary is someone legally obligated to act in your best interests. This commitment is not just an ethical standard but a legal one, which can make a significant difference in the quality of advice you receive.

Why is having a fiduciary so valuable? It's simple: a fiduciary's decisions must prioritize your benefit over their own. If your financial advisor is not a fiduciary, they're held to a less stringent standard of care, which can lead to conflicts of interest between what's best for you and what benefits them financially.

Some advisors may choose not to be fiduciaries, possibly due to their compensation models or a desire to avoid legal responsibilities. Non-fiduciary advisors might be less accountable for their advice, with fewer repercussions for actions that don't align with your best interest.

It's essential to understand how your advisor is compensated. Fiduciary advisors are typically transparent about their fees—how they are paid and how their fees are calculated. This transparency is a cornerstone of trust in the client-advisor relationship.

Non-fiduciaries often work on a commission-based model, earning money from the financial products they sell to you. While not all commission-based advisors are unethical, the potential for conflict of interest is higher. For example, an advisor may recommend a Class A share mutual fund that pays a substantial commission upfront but restricts your ability to move your investment without incurring additional charges. This limitation can lead to a stagnant strategy, even when better investment opportunities exist elsewhere.

Similarly, a stockbroker who earns commissions on trades has an incentive to encourage more buying and selling, regardless of whether it's in your long-term financial interest. The more trades, the more they earn, which could lead to unnecessary transactions that benefit the advisor more than you.

In contrast, a fiduciary advisor, who typically earns a management fee, aligns their success with yours. They manage your investments proactively, making decisions based on a pre-agreed strategy, not on a transactional basis. Their fee model incentivizes them to grow your wealth, as their compensation is a direct result of your portfolio's performance.

In summary, it is not just about the advice but also about the advisor's motivation. Knowing how your financial advisor is compensated is a critical aspect of your financial well-being. This knowledge helps you assess whether their advice is genuinely intended to serve your interests. Transparency in compensation models promotes accountability, and following the money can often reveal an advisor's true priorities. Choose wisely. Your financial future may depend on it.

CHAPTER FOUR

RISK and REWARD
You Can't Have One Without the Other

In the sixties, Frank Sinatra sang a song about the link between love and marriage and how you can't have one without the other. The two are linked.

Today, some might say it's a dated concept, which is an argument for another day.

For the purpose of investing for retirement, there is no argument about the inseparable link between risk and reward.

The potential reward you might get from any investment is linked to the degree of risk of investment loss that the instrument exposes us to.

It may be helpful to consider this relationship between risk and reward as a pyramid. This pyramid contains the entire world of choices where money can be invested: stocks, bonds, real estate, gold, crypto, bank CDs, or even cash.

REWARD — RISK

The specific location where each of these instruments would be located on this pyramid is based on the degree of the potential reward each offers and the degree of potential risk of loss that each might expose us to.

Before investing any of your hard-earned savings, the best thing to understand is that this link between risk and reward is unbreakable.

Anytime you hear a promoter offering an investment that they say will make you a lot of money with no risk, I want you to be cautious.

The fluctuations in the cryptocurrency market exemplify the intricate relationship between risk and reward. The price history of Bitcoin starkly illustrates this connection. For instance, an investment in one Bitcoin in the summer of 2020, when the price was under $10,000, could have yielded a substantial profit if sold when the price surged to about $60,000 less than a year later. Such a considerable increase exemplifies the high-reward aspect of cryptocurrency investment.

Conversely, the risk element is highlighted by the subsequent price movement, where someone purchasing Bitcoin at its peak in 2021 for $60,000 would have seen its value plummet to less than $20,000 by the summer of 2022. Although the price partially recovered to approximately $40,000 when this was written, the future trajectory of Bitcoin's value remains uncertain, underscoring the volatility and inherent risks associated with cryptocurrency investments.

This volatility is why, in an investment strategy, cryptocurrencies would be positioned at the apex of an investment pyramid, symbolizing their status as assets with high potential for both significant risk and substantial reward. The point is not to pass judgment on the merit of cryptocurrencies as an investment choice but to categorize them according to their risk-reward profile, which is among the highest in the investment landscape.

Savings kept in cash or cash equivalents like bank savings accounts, Treasure bills, or money market funds deserve a spot at the bottom of the pyramid. There is little, if any, risk of investment loss, but the rewards in terms of interest earnings are small or even zero.

While stock and stock market-type investments reside higher up on this pyramid, the location of a well-diversified stock portfolio would appropriately be lower than Crypto.

Based on historical performance, it would be difficult to find many knowledgeable investors who would expect the values in the S&P 500 index to swing as wildly as crypto has over such short periods.

Every investment can have a different position on this pyramid, but what doesn't change is that while the degree of reward to risk will be either higher or lower, the connection is unbreakable.

The question is: How do we manage or balance the various degrees of risk of investment loss along with the inflation and longevity risk we potentially face?

The Reality of Retirement Planning: No Magical Solutions

The adage "You can't pull a rabbit out of a hat" resonates profoundly among retirement planners. It reflects the truth that there is no miraculous fix for your savings or a shortcut to catch up if you're behind. Some believe aggressively playing the stock market might offer a quick solution, but such tactics are fraught with risks and can potentially worsen your financial situation.

Acceptance is the first step. Recognize that what you've saved is what you have to work with. This sum, however much it may be, is the foundation upon which your financial plan must be built—a plan that should incorporate thoughtful risk management and a realistic assessment of your financial situation.

Once acceptance is in place, it's time to strategize. Crafting a retirement plan involves making significant choices about how you wish to spend your later years. It's about confronting the reality of your savings and asking yourself what you want your retirement to look like. Do you crave the freedom and possibilities that come with leaving the workforce, or are you content to continue your current routine?

This is an invitation to embrace the fruits of your labor and proceed with life on your terms, armed with the knowledge that, while there's no magical fix, you can still make empowering choices. It may require adjusting expectations and finding contentment within the means you have.

I often emphasize that a fulfilling retirement isn't measured by the amount of money you spend but rather by how you spend your life. There's a certain liberation in acknowledging that while you cannot change the past, you can influence your future. Retirement should be a time to enjoy life's journey with the resources you've gathered. It's time to set out on this next adventure with confidence and make the most of the years ahead.

Understanding Your Investments: The Importance of Knowledge

A cornerstone of financial empowerment is the principle: "Know what you own and why you own it." Education is the key that unlocks confidence and conviction in your financial decisions. It's what enables you to adhere to your personal financial plan even when the market is volatile.

Knowing what you own and why isn't just about being able to list your assets—it's about understanding the role each investment plays in your portfolio. Whether it's stocks, bonds, cash, annuities, or any other form of investment, you should be able to articulate why each one is part of your strategy.

In my practice, I've observed a common gap: many individuals arrive without a clear explanation for their investment choices. My goal is always to bridge this gap, to ensure that by the time you leave my office, you not only know what you own but also appreciate how each asset contributes to achieving your financial goals. This knowledge is the foundation upon which a resilient financial plan is built.

Pause for a moment and consider this: Shouldn't you fully know the reasons behind each asset in your possession? It's essential to grasp the purpose behind holding a particular asset to be genuinely invested in your financial plan. Remember, this is your capital—take ownership of your financial decisions.

To illustrate, imagine you come into my office with several annuities and a brokerage statement. When reviewing these annuities and discussing your financial situation, I might ask why you chose to invest in these particular products and how they fit into your broader financial plan. Often, I hear a variety of responses. Unfortunately, more often than not, they aren't reasons; they're rationalizations for a purchase made in the past.

The next step is to understand, at least in basic terms, how these annuities function, what type they are, and why you're holding them. Various explanations may emerge, and that's okay. However, in my experience, people often admit they bought them out of fear of market risk because their advisor recommended it, or sometimes they can't articulate a reason at all. This lack of understanding is problematic. It's crucial that you thoroughly comprehend the rationale behind the acquisition of any financial product, such as annuities. Your economic well-being depends on informed decisions, which require a clear understanding of your investments.

Annuities can be a strategic component in a diversified portfolio, aligned with specific financial goals and suitable for particular investors. Like any financial tool, I incorporate annuities into a client's portfolio only when they serve as the right solution to a defined need. An inappropriate purchase is one made without understanding its purpose, as in the case where someone buys an annuity solely for the appeal of no market risk without grasping its role in their financial plan.

For instance, if a well-informed client of mine, let's call him Tom, is questioned by a friend or colleague about his purchase of an annuity, the explanation would be comprehensive and tied to his unique financial strategy. The conversation might go something like this:

"Tom, I've heard annuities have drawbacks. Why did you opt for one?"

Tom would reply, "Jim, I invested in an annuity because it's a calculated part of my overall retirement plan. It's a deliberate choice we made for my income strategy. Specifically, it's a cornerstone of my 'Bucket #1'—the segment of my portfolio that's tasked with providing a reliable stream of income in retirement. This annuity sits in my 'lifestyle bucket,' furnishing me with a safe and stable income, which is crucial for shielding me from economic uncertainties. It ensures that my basic financial needs are met, allowing me to live confidently without worrying about my essentials. Additionally, this annuity lowers the risk profile of my entire portfolio, giving me the freedom to invest other assets in opportunities with higher growth potential, which I believe will benefit me in the long term."

This response exemplifies a client's understanding of their financial choices, demonstrating the importance of purposeful and informed investment decisions.

Grasping the "why" behind each investment is crucial to ensuring your financial plan is coherent and tailored to your needs. When considering an annuity or any financial product, clarity on its role in your overall strategy is essential. Let's consider how this understanding plays out in a real-life scenario:

Imagine a client, Tom, who's been asked about his investment choices, particularly regarding annuities and stocks, in the context of his age and retirement plans.

When questioned about his annuity holdings, Tom has a clear explanation:

"I chose annuities because they align with my financial goals. I understand their function within my portfolio, ensuring I purchase them for the right reasons. It's part of my strategy for predictable retirement income, fitting seamlessly into my financial plan."

Now, shifting to stocks, the conversation might unfold as follows:

"Tom, isn't investing in stocks too risky at your age, especially when retired?"

Tom responds confidently, "I own stocks as an integral element of my financial plan, and they serve a specific purpose for my future. Stocks are assigned to 'Bucket #3' in my investment strategy, which is earmarked for growth and managed risk. This bucket is designed for long-term growth and is not intended for immediate income needs. With my

'Bucket #1' safeguarding my lifestyle with secure income and 'Bucket #2' covering additional income needs with lower risk, I can afford to allocate risk to my third bucket. This growth is essential for potential health expenses, combating inflation, and enhancing future income. I'm aware of the risks, but they are calculated and purposeful. That's why, even at my age, stocks are a sensible part of my plan."

Tom's replies highlight the importance of knowing not just what you own but why you own it. This knowledge is fundamental to staying engaged with your financial strategy, fostering confidence, and understanding in the investment decisions made to achieve your goals. Every portion of the investment portfolio is planned with a clear objective and a defined role, contributing to the overall success of your financial journey.

When Enough Is Enough

Acknowledging when you've reached your financial goals is as crucial as setting them. Reflecting on "when is enough, enough?" helps you understand your actual financial needs versus chasing arbitrary benchmarks set by external influences.

Consider the concept of "enough." It's a fundamental question that's often overlooked. Many people, perhaps unconsciously, pursue an elusive figure they believe is required for retirement, influenced by media or societal expectations. This chase can lead to a sense of never having enough, overshadowing the achievements and savings you've already amassed.

Rather than fixating on some abstract number, I advise my clients to focus on what they realistically need for retirement.

The key is understanding your retirement goals and lifestyle expectations and then tailoring your savings to meet those specific objectives. It's not about hitting a certain number because someone else says it's right. It's about knowing your personal "enough"—that sweet spot where your savings align with your life's aspirations. This approach prevents you from unnecessary risks; why gamble more than what's required to secure your desired retirement?

Understanding what drives you in life is essential for meaningful financial planning. It's about taking a moment to ask yourself the deeper questions: What are my true desires? Is it a hunger for change, the urge to explore different paths, or the aspiration to engage more with family and loved ones? Maybe it's the dream to travel to distant lands or simply enjoy the comfort of your home without the stress of work.

Money and net worth are tools that can help fulfill these dreams. Yet, achieving fulfillment starts with clarity about what those dreams are. Before chasing after financial goals, it's crucial to identify what you're chasing and why.

Have you considered what's genuinely important to you beyond the societal benchmarks of success? Perhaps it's not about a bigger house or a luxury car but about the freedom to live life on your terms. This personal insight is what should guide your financial targets.

With this understanding, you can gauge whether your ambitions are within financial reach. It may turn out that your current resources are more than adequate to cover what will genuinely make you content. Or you may find that you need to adjust your financial strategies to bridge the gap between your dreams and reality.

This approach shifts the focus from accumulating wealth for its own sake to building and using wealth as a means to an end. The end being a life rich in experiences and relationships that are most valuable to you. Only by identifying and embracing your aspirations can you align your financial planning with your life's purpose.

After many years of working with clients, I've observed that individuals often struggle to pinpoint their own wants and needs. The dedication to serving others—through careers, nurturing families, and raising children—often eclipses the practice of self-reflection. Consequently, when the time comes to contemplate one's desires for the remainder of life, it can seem like an unfamiliar, even overwhelming task.

Once clarity is reached regarding what constitutes an ideal retirement, the focus can pivot to the essential monthly income that will make that scenario a reality. The conversation should transition from net worth to the more pertinent topic of income requirements.

The primary principle to remember is the precedence of income. In our earning years, we utilize our income for expenses. Upon retirement, the source of income shifts, yet the fundamental concept remains unchanged. The retirement funds must be repurposed to generate a consistent, monthly "paycheck" to maintain our lifestyles.

This generated income is the key to freedom in retirement. With assets providing for your needs, spending time earning a wage is less necessary, freeing you up for other pursuits. This liberation can open doors to activities like volunteer work, crafting a legacy, or engaging in hobbies.

A secure and predictable income stream gives one the confidence to look beyond the basics and fulfill more profound aspirations. It might sound straightforward, but realizing this requires substantial thought. Taking the time to absorb this concept is vital. It's not merely about ensuring we can live comfortably but about empowering ourselves to live meaningfully. This reflective process is crucial in aligning one's financial strategy with life's ambitions, enabling a focus on personal fulfillment and broader contributions to society.

We've reached an insightful juncture on our financial journey, and I encourage you to pause and ponder what you desire and the avenues through which you can realize those aspirations. The threshold of "enough" is crossed when our accrued monthly income can breathe life into our dreams. Our financial success isn't encapsulated by the figures on our bank statements but rather by the income they can generate.

Should we fret if our ideal wants remain just beyond our grasp? Many exhaust their lives in pursuit of elusive goals. Instead, embracing what we've already attained can be a springboard for embarking on new adventures. It's not the numerical milestones but the richness of life that should guide our pursuit. This moment calls for introspection and an honest evaluation of our deepest objectives. Today marks the starting point for such a transformative exercise.

This realization is liberating. Why? Because it reflects a conscious choice. We're directing our lives and finances with purpose, opting for personal fulfillment over impersonal targets. The relentless race for more becomes redundant once you've gathered sufficient resources to satisfy your wishes. Acknowledging this achievement is crucial—allow yourself to relish in the fruits of your labor.

If there's uncertainty about whether your retirement funds suffice for your ambitions, a pivotal decision looms. This choice has profound implications. Is more truly necessary? Here, the importance of focused and deliberate planning is evident. Dedicate time to determine the retirement income necessary for your preferred lifestyle and measure it against what your assets are likely to yield. If there's a gap, assess whether the sacrifices needed to bridge it are worth the trade-off.

Throughout my experience guiding numerous clients into retirement, one insight stands out: Few invest adequate time in self-reflection and personal contentment. Now presents an opportunity to make that pivotal decision: is enough truly enough? Be bold and turn your intentions into reality.

The Importance of Understanding Your Personal Tolerance for Investment Risk

Understanding your risk tolerance is a pivotal aspect of financial planning. As we delve into the nuances of risk, it's crucial not only to recognize the risks you're taking but also to comprehend the underlying reasons. This is the juncture at which envisioning your financial future becomes essential. My experience has led me to believe that our risk tendencies often stem from a lack of education. We're seldom taught to appreciate how risk interplays with our financial strategies.

Why emphasize the creation of a vision? It's about formulating a clear and tangible picture of your goals— understanding what you're working towards and where you aspire to be financially. This foresight is not just motivational; it's strategic.

Being risk-averse and opting for minimal risk can seem like the comfortable choice, and it might align with your financial plan—or it might not. By crafting a clear vision of our financial destination, we might find that embracing a certain level of risk is not just beneficial but necessary to achieve our objectives.

Consider a scenario where you're forty years old with a notably low-risk tolerance. You're aiming for a comfortable retirement fund to support your aspirations but feel overwhelmed by market downturns, like the one during the COVID-19 pandemic and the economic turbulence marked by high inflation and rising interest rates in 2022. These events have shaken your confidence, and you question the value of taking any risk. In this case, your immediate reactions to short-term market fluctuations overshadow your investment strategy's long-term perspective. Essentially, you're allowing one or a few turbulent years to influence your approach for the next couple of decades.

To navigate this, examining the historical performance of different investment allocations or benchmarks is crucial. A key question arises: At what age do you aim to retire, and what monthly income will you need to sustain your lifestyle? Recalling our previous discussions, these details are significant. For our forty-year-old, with a retirement target of sixty-five, there's a twenty-five-year investment window to consider.

For clarity, let's briefly look at two hypothetical benchmarks: a balanced portfolio comprising 50 percent stocks and 50 percent bonds and the S&P 500 index, representing a stock market benchmark. Comparing these could provide a glimpse into what the potential retirement fund might look like years down the line. However, remember these figures are purely illustrative and not to be relied upon for actual investment decisions.

Understanding your risk tolerance is crucial, as it has a significant impact on potential investment outcomes. With twenty-five years to plan, assessing various rates of return and applying them to see the projected final balance is a vital exercise.

To illustrate using Kwanti software analysis, let's examine two portfolios: a 50/50 mix of the S&P 500 index and the AGG aggregate bond index and the S&P 500 index alone. Historically, over a rolling twenty-five-year period, the 50/50 portfolio might have returned an annualized rate of around 6.06 percent, while the S&P 500 could have yielded approximately 7.97 percent. That's a notable difference of 1.91 percent.

At first glance, this difference might seem minor, and considering the higher risk associated with the S&P 500 index, one might question if it's worth it. This is where it becomes essential to visualize the future you're striving for and determine if taking on additional risk aligns with that vision. By understanding the reasoning behind risk-taking, you can make more informed decisions that reflect your comfort level and financial goals.

Let's delve into the tangible impact of risk tolerance over the long term with an example. Suppose you've saved $250,000 at age forty and plan to contribute $15,000 annually towards retirement. Let's discern the difference that an extra 1.91 percent in returns could potentially make over twenty-five years.

For the 50/50 portfolio, with an assumed return of 6.06 percent, the projected value of your savings could reach around $1,918,210. Quite impressive. Now, looking at the S&P 500 Index with a hypothetical return of 7.97 percent, the future value could be approximately $2,792,064. That's a substantial difference of $873,854.[1]

When you envision your financial future, which balance would you prefer? Would the discomfort caused by short-term market downturns be worth foregoing nearly $874,000 over a quarter of a century? This is a clear illustration of why it's imperative not to let short-term fluctuations derail your long-term financial strategy.

---

1   Calculation derived from Dinkytown.Net: Financial Calculators. https://www.dinkytown.net/java/future-value-calculator.html

With this perspective, the reason for embracing risk becomes more concrete: it could potentially be worth $873,854 to you. It helps in visualizing the long-term benefits and steeling yourself during volatile periods, understanding that knee-jerk reactions to market dips could be incredibly costly.

Simultaneously, it's just as important to recognize when risk-taking might exceed your comfort level or financial capacity, leading into the crucial discussion of balancing risk with prudence.

Don't Take Chances with Income

It's a widespread belief that to reach our financial aspirations, we must engage in greater risk, continually chasing after elusive returns. This pursuit is underpinned by the undeniable power of compound interest, which, with higher returns, can significantly amplify wealth over time—this is an indisputable financial truth. However, as we explored in Chapter Four, the journey toward higher returns invariably intertwines with increased risk.

In the realm of investment losses, our North Star should be the pursuit of our return objectives while navigating around the stormy seas of risk whenever possible. The art of investment isn't just about the gains; it's equally about how deftly you can sidestep the pitfalls. That's why our retirement planning begins not with a gamble for higher stakes but with a calculated approach to enhance returns without pushing our savings into the tumultuous tides of additional risk.

A key objective woven into our financial plans is eliminating unnecessary risk. It's akin to preparing for a voyage—not by bracing for every possible storm but by choosing a route that avoids them where we can. This doesn't mean our journey is without risk—navigating entirely in calm waters is rarely possible. Assets earmarked for retirement invariably require growth to secure your future shore.

Yet, my philosophy holds that while some measure of risk may be necessary to achieve required growth, it must be prudent, well measured, and, above all, necessary.

In my seasoned judgment, safeguarding income against excessive risk is a cornerstone of sound financial planning. When protecting your income from too much risk, it's essential to look out for two main types: the risk from changing interest rates and the risk from unpredictable markets. Most people know that market risk is all about the ups and downs in investment prices. However, not everyone is as familiar with interest rate risk, which is a big deal for bonds—both the kind companies issue and those issued by the government.

Often, investors are advised to put some of their money into bonds. This is a way to spread out their risks and make sure not all their eggs are in one basket. It is a solid strategy but gets tricky when you need to start using your investments as a source of income during retirement. Let's take a look at the AGG bond index as an example. This index keeps track of high-quality bonds in the U.S. Let's say you put half your money into AGG because you've been told it's a smart move for spreading out your risks.

Now, rewind to March 2022. The Federal Reserve started raising interest rates to fight off high inflation. When interest rates go up, bond values tend to go down. By October 2022, AGG saw its value drop by about 18 percent from where it was at its highest. That's interest rate risk in action.

Think about someone who's retired and needs money from their investments to live on. AGG's returns for the years 2021, 2022, and up to October 2023 were down by -1.77 percent, -13.03 percent, and -1.8 percent. These drops mean less money coming in. And it gets worse if you've also put the other half of your money into the stock market, which we saw with the S&P 500 index losing 20 percent in 2022.

This all means that even bonds, which many people think of as safer places to put their money, come with risks that you need to keep an eye on, especially if you depend on your investments for retirement income. Building a portfolio that can give you steady money in retirement means being smart about all these risks, not just the ones in the stock market.

Think back to the first bucket we talked about before. The whole point of that bucket is to ensure there's no risk to your investment income. So, if you put a portion of your money into something steady like a fixed indexed annuity, you wouldn't have to worry about changing interest rates or ups and downs in the market affecting your money. This step helps remove risks we don't need to take and makes your financial plan more secure. It's all about ensuring you have a reliable income no matter what's happening in the economy.

The Importance of Time-Horizon

Time is a crucial ally in mitigating the risks of investment losses, particularly in the stock market. For the younger investor, time affords the luxury to remain steadfast during market downturns. Historically, markets have demonstrated a tendency to recover and advance over time, allowing investors to weather the inevitable fluctuations.

A common adage about the market is that it tends to "take three steps forward and one step back." Consider the period from 2000 to 2002 when the market experienced a significant downturn, plummeting over 47 percent from peak to trough before rebounding in 2007. Then came the 2008 financial crisis, with the S&P 500 tumbling over 37 percent and the market not recovering until March 2009, representing a drop of over 53 percent. From 2009 to 2022, the market saw no drawdowns exceeding 20 percent.

Reflect on this: from 2000 to 2020, the S&P 500 faced three major downturns exceeding 30 percent. Yet, for someone who was thirty in 2000 and reached fifty by 2020, there was ample time to endure these downturns and still benefit from long-term growth. To provide a broader perspective, including dividends and after adjusting for inflation, the S&P 500 index averaged an annual return of more than 7 percent during this twenty year period. This illustrates that with patience and the passage of time, the market's upward trajectory has historically prevailed despite short-term setbacks.

Understanding the impact of market volatility is pivotal, particularly when juxtaposing the investing stages of accumulation with the cusp of retirement. If you are at an age where your investment strategy does not require tapping into your savings, you have the capacity to endure market downturns to potentially reap higher returns later. However, the scenario dramatically shifts if you are nearing retirement.

Imagine being on the verge of retirement and witnessing a plunge in your portfolio of over 30 percent or even the extreme 53 percent witnessed during the 2007-2009 financial crisis. The discomfort would be palpable. It's a common refrain to hear that "the market always recovers," with many citing the post-2008 recovery as a testament to a hands-off approach. But this perspective changes with age. If you were unaffected in 2008 because you were years away from needing your investments for income, that's one thing. Fast forward to 2023, if you're now at retirement age, the picture is starkly different. You might no longer have the luxury of waiting for a recovery without financial strain.

It's imperative to recognize that each individual's financial blueprint and lifestyle demands are unique. Not everyone can comfortably ride out a significant market dip, especially if they rely heavily on their investment portfolio for income during retirement. Those who don't need the funds and are investing with the intention of leaving a legacy may have the resilience to withstand market downturns.

For others, such volatility could jeopardize their income strategy and overall financial stability. If your circumstances mean that a severe market drop would derail your financial plans, it's crucial to reassess your investment approach to align with your current life stage and income needs.

Grasping the nuances of income requirements in retirement is essential. First, you must understand what you'll need financially in retirement and then tailor your investment risk accordingly. When you begin to draw down from your retirement savings, it's crucial that this doesn't adversely impact the lifestyle you've worked hard to attain. Most people don't envision a retirement where they must return to work out of necessity rather than choice.

Consider this scenario to illustrate my point: I advocate for a no-risk approach to the income you need immediately. Risk should be reserved for capital that is earmarked for the future. Suppose you have a $500,000 portfolio and adhere to the "set it and forget it" philosophy, trusting in the market because that's what you've been taught.

Moreover, assume you subscribe to the 4 percent withdrawal rule, a principle formulated by William Bengen. This rule is a well-known retirement strategy that proposes that retirees can withdraw 4 percent of their retirement pot in their first year of retirement and adjust for inflation each year after that, aiming to sustain their funds for thirty years.

Aligning your portfolio's risk level with your income needs ensures that you won't have to compromise your lifestyle or face the prospect of returning to work when you should be enjoying your retirement.

Embark on this thought journey: you've decided to strictly adhere to the 4 percent withdrawal rule for retirement, investing your savings in the S&P 500 index. Now, picture beginning this approach in January 1999. Fast forward through time, and you'll observe a disturbing trend. By the time you reach the age of eighty-five, twenty years later, your finances have dwindled to nothing. Some may argue that such an outcome is highly unusual, but history tells us these events are possible and could reoccur.

Month	Year	Beginning Value	One-Year Index Return	Change in Value	Annual Withdrawal	Year End Value
January	1999	$500,000	8.91%	$44,550	$20,000	$524,550
January	2000	$524,550	-2.01%	($10,543)	$20,600	$493,407
January	2001	$493,407	-17.28%	($85,261)	$21,218	$386,928
January	2002	$386,928	-24.25%	($93,830)	$21,855	$271,243
January	2003	$271,243	32.13%	$87,150	$22,511	$335,882
January	2004	$335,882	4.42%	$14,846	$23,186	$327,542
January	2005	$327,542	8.38%	$27,448	$23,882	$331,108
January	2006	$331,108	12.34%	$40,859	$24,598	$347,369
January	2007	$347,369	-4.10%	($14,242)	$25,336	$307,791
January	2008	$307,791	-40.10%	($123,424)	$26,096	$158,271
January	2009	$158,271	30.02%	$47,513	$26,879	$178,905
January	2010	$178,905	19.74%	$35,316	$27,685	$186,536
January	2011	$186,536	0.47%	$877	$28,516	$158,897
January	2012	$158,897	15.94%	$25,328	$29,371	$154,854
January	2013	$154,854	18.96%	$29,360	$30,252	$153,962
January	2014	$153,962	11.95%	$18,398	$31,160	$141,200
January	2015	$141,200	-2.76%	($3,897)	$32,095	$105,208
January	2016	$105,208	17.42%	$18,327	$33,058	$90,477
January	2017	$90,477	23.92%	$21,642	$34,050	$78,069
January	2018	$78,069	-4.22%	($3,295)	$35,072	$39,702
January	2019	$39,702	19.27%	$7,651	$36,124	$11,229
Total Change in Account Value: 97.75%						

Prepared By: Chris Mediate
Mediate Financial Services, Inc.

The purpose of this illustration is to demonstrate the potential risks of depleting an account when annual withdrawals are combined with market volatility. This illustration shows hypothetical results of an account invested in a broad stock market index and does not account for the re-investment of dividends or any investment fees associated with an account. The index values used for the calculations are month-end closing values that are adjusted for dividends and splits and were obtained from Yahoo Finance. Calculations assume deferral of taxes. The Standard & Poors 500 (S&P 500) is an unmanaged group of securities considered to be representative of the stock market in general. The Dow Jones Industrial Average (DJIA) is a price-weighted average of thirty significant stocks traded on the New York Stock Exchange.

You might think, "Well, I"ll just reduce my withdrawals when the market's down to prevent depleting my savings." But consider this: you have devoted years to hard work, saving diligently for retirement, and now you may have to compromise your lifestyle simply because you chose not to adapt your risk profile. This exemplifies why it's so crucial to be mindful of your time horizon and risk tolerance.

As for the 4 percent rule, my views are reserved for a deeper discussion on bucket planning. Your income plan should be as unique as you are, tailored to where you're drawing your money from, and aligned with your lifestyle. It shouldn't be a one-size-fits-all approach. If the 4 percent rule aligns with your situation, it's essential to understand the intricacies of how and from where you're distributing your funds. The importance of a personalized plan will become even clearer in the following chapter.

The 100-Minus Age Rule

The 100-Minus Age Rule is a traditional heuristic in the world of investing, suggesting that you subtract your age from 100 to find the percentage of your portfolio that should be invested in stocks. For instance, if you're fifty years old, the formula implies a 50 percent investment in stocks, whereas at fifty-eight, it suggests 42 percent.

However, from my perspective, this rule should serve merely as a preliminary gauge of your investment temperament. It's a generalized strategy, not a definitive mandate. Consider a forty-year-old by this rule: 60 percent of their portfolio would be in stocks. Yet, this allocation might not reflect their actual risk appetite or financial objectives. That's why I view this rule as a conversational icebreaker rather than a rigid principle.

Your investment strategy should be tailored to your unique risk tolerance and dovetail with your goals and life plan. Remember, this financial journey is yours and yours alone, so it's critical that the decisions you make resonate with your objectives. If your aim is to amplify your wealth, as outlined in the earlier discussion about aligning your risk appetite with appropriate benchmarks, then a heftier allocation towards stocks might be justified. Conversely, as you mature in years, the proportion of risk you assign to stock investments should be carefully calibrated to the specifics of your financial blueprint. Risk is not a one-size-fits-all concept; it must be measured against the backdrop of your income strategy and the broader picture of your financial aspirations. Essentially, it's about forging a path that reflects your circumstances, not a path paved by over simplified financial maxims.

The concept of risk versus reward is highly personalized and central to crafting a financial strategy that is truly your own. There is no universal blueprint that can be indiscriminately applied to everyone's financial situation because each individual's needs and circumstances are unique. It's essential to understand how to evaluate benchmarks properly, to assess the risk of potential declines (drawdowns) in your investments, and to consider how these align with your requirements for income and your time horizon for investing.

By embracing these principles, you can create a financial plan that not only reflects but also respects the nuances of your life goals and risk appetite. This tailored approach ensures that your plan is not a product of arbitrary rules but a result of carefully considering what works best for you.

CHAPTER FIVE

Your Savings' Mission: Income
Determining How Much and for How Long

You can't enjoy retirement unless you have vitality. But when I say vitality, I am not referring to the physical state of being strong and in excellent health. Instead, I am talking about the "vital organ" of retirement, which is income. You can't exist without the vital organ of your heart pumping blood throughout your body, just like you can't truly live an enjoyable, fulfilling retirement without the essential organ of income.

How Much Income Will I Need?

The primary purpose of your savings and investing in your retirement accounts is to provide the income you'll need to cover the ebbs and flows of retirement spending. But this leads to the critical question almost every retiree asks: "What is a safe spending rate that ensures my savings last throughout retirement?"

Answering this question requires finding a delicate equilibrium. On one side, there's the desire to indulge in the rewards of your hard work, pursue lifelong dreams, and savor the leisure of retirement. On the flip side, you face the tangible worry of exhausting your savings prematurely, potentially leaving you financially vulnerable in your advanced years.

Navigating this balance begins with a deeper understanding of the predictable patterns of spending you'll likely encounter during retirement.

A Dangerous Retirement Planning Rule of Thumb

When you sit down to talk retirement with a broker or financial advisor, there's a familiar script you're likely to encounter. It often hinges on a simple "replacement rate" concept, suggesting you'll need about 70 to 90 percent of your pre-retirement income once you retire, followed up by annual increases to cover the inflation rate.

If we view this spending pattern as a line on a graph, it might look something like this.

However, through my thirty years as a financial advisor, guiding hundreds through the transition into retirement, I've come to question this

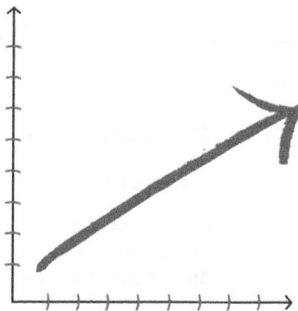

standard advice. My professional experience shows a different picture: many retirees don't immediately cut back on spending. In fact, quite the opposite is true. The early years of retirement are often marked by increased spending as retirees finally embark on long-awaited travels or dive into hobbies and interests that were sidelined during their working years. Retirement opens up a new chapter brimming with potential and choices.

This observation isn't just based on anecdotes. It's supported by scholarly research, like the study from the Michigan Retirement and Disability Research Center at the University of Michigan. Their investigation into retirees' spending habits confirmed what I've seen in the field. When retirees were asked about their spending over the past six years, the majority didn't report the expected decrease. Only 29 percent noticed a reduction in their spending. A substantial 37 percent saw no change at all, and a significant 34 percent even experienced increased expenditures.[2] These findings challenge the typical narrative and suggest a need for a more nuanced approach to retirement planning.

As retirees advance into their seventies, a notable shift in spending patterns often occurs. The question arises: What prompts this change from the initial freedom of spending to a more cautious approach? For some, this shift is a reaction

---

2   Susann Rohweddar, "Explanations for the Decline in Spending at Older Ages." June 2022. Michigan Retirement and Disability Research Center. https://mrdrc.isr.umich.edu/publications/papers/pdf/wp440.pdf

to their retirement savings decreasing faster than anticipated, sounding financial alarms.

However, there's another distinct narrative for many
retirees. This group isn't dialing back their expenses out
of financial necessity, but rather, they're choosing a more
modest lifestyle. Their reasons are varied and extend beyond
the state of their finances.

Consider travel, a common indulgence among the
young-at-heart retirees aged sixty-five to sixty-nine. That
age range is the golden era of retirement, often characterized by a zest for adventure and exploration. Yet, as they
progress into their seventies, a noticeable downturn in
travel spending typically occurs. This isn't necessarily due
to financial constraints. More often, it reflects the onset of
health-related limitations, with one or both partners facing
challenges that make travel less enjoyable or too strenuous.
The decline in travel isn't because the dream destinations
like Mediterranean cruises or African safaris are suddenly
unaffordable. It's that the value and pleasure derived from
these experiences diminish due to health considerations.

This trend serves as a poignant reminder of the tran-
sient nature of good health and the unpredictability it brings
to our lives. It's a call to action for new retirees: Embrace
and make the most of the early retirement years. It's wise
to meticulously plan for the future, but it's just as critical to
live vibrantly in the present. The early retirement years are

precious, and pursuing your passions and dreams with vigor is essential, as our health and ability to enjoy such pursuits may not be as certain in later years.

As we grow older, there's a natural decline in spending for activities like travel, dining out, and other recreational pursuits. However, it's important to anticipate and plan for the likelihood of increased spending on healthcare and long-term care services towards the latter part of life. Statistics suggest that approximately 70 percent of older adults in the United States will require some form of long-term care.[3]

Discussing long-term care requires expanding our view beyond the conventional image of nursing homes. A considerable proportion of such care is provided in the comfort of one's home or within community-based settings like adult daycare centers and assisted living facilities. Let's delve into what this might mean financially:

- Receiving in-home care typically costs around $60,000 per year.
- Opting for an assisted living facility will cost roughly the same, at about $59,000 annually.
- If the level of care escalates to that of a nursing home, the annual costs significantly increase, exceeding $100,000 for a private room.[4]

3   Barbara Marquand. "Long-Term Care Insurance Explained." Nerdwallet. July 7, 2023. https://www.nerdwallet.com/article/insurance/long-term-care-insurance

4   Nationwide Financial. 2022. https://nationwidefinacialltcmap.hvsfinancial.com/

SMILE

From a broad perspective, envisioning the typical pattern of retirement spending wouldn't look like a straight line on a graph. It's more akin to the curve of a smile.

Initially, retirees often experience a spike in spending, indulging in long-awaited pleasures like globe-trotting or epic road trips. As they enter their seventies, there's a noticeable decline in discretionary expenses for many. Yet, it's crucial to note that towards the latter part of retirement, spending tends to rise again due to escalating medical and long-term care costs.

This ebb and flow in spending underscores the need for comprehensive retirement planning. Such planning should reflect the energetic early retirement years, the calmer middle phase, and the later years that might see increased healthcare expenditures. Preparing with this nuanced understanding of spending trends equips you with the financial resilience to navigate through all stages of retirement confidently.

How Long Will I Need Income?

Let's take a journey back in time to perhaps a familiar scenario, be it through the experiences of your grandparents, your parents, or your own. There was a time when loyalty to a job was commonplace. Often, a single employer would be the hallmark of one's career. This fidelity was not taken lightly; it was born out of a memory of more challenging times, like the Great Depression, where a job wasn't just a job—it was the bedrock of a family's security.

Employers, in turn, acknowledged this loyalty by setting aside funds for their employees. After years of service, employees were rewarded with a pension upon retirement—a guaranteed income stream to sustain them through their non-working years. This was more than just a benefit; it was a vital piece of the financial puzzle, ensuring that even though work stops, living costs do not. The pension was the creation of income for the future, an anchor of financial stability in a sea of uncertainties.

Upon submitting their retirement notice, employees were once celebrated with a symbolic gold watch, marking three decades of dedication. This wasn't merely a token of appreciation but the prelude to a new chapter. With the turn of the next month, the tangible reward of their labor arrived in their mailboxes—a pension check, a piece of certainty in a world of variables. It was a symbol of security, a source of gratitude, for it meant they could continue to provide for themselves and their families, unwinding from the years of hard work. The importance of this system lay in its reliability; the income would persist for the entirety of their lives, often extending to support their spouse in their absence. The assurance that—even at ninety-five—the checks would continue was invaluable.

Fast forward to today, and the landscape has shifted dramatically. Pensions have become the "dinosaurs" of the financial world—rare, remarkable, and sadly, on the brink of extinction. Those who are recipients of such benefits should indeed consider themselves fortunate. Pensions represent more than just income; they are synonymous with longevity and spousal protection, a beacon of safety and stability in the uncertain seas of financial planning.

Speak to retired teachers or auto workers about their pensions, and you'll likely hear a common sentiment: It is their lifeline. Today's narrative has changed; workers bear the onus of securing their retirements more than ever. They find themselves navigating the complex terrain of savings and investment vehicles like 401(k)s, attempting to accumulate enough wealth not only to retire but to determine a strategy for its utilization. The questions are ceaseless and daunting: How much is sufficient? How much can safely be withdrawn each year? Will it last? What happens upon my passing? Will my spouse be secure? The certainty once provided by pensions is now a tapestry of individual responsibility and planning, where each worker must become their own architect of retirement security.

I understand completely, as these are the concerns I encounter daily. The need for clear, definitive answers is pressing. The bigger picture is becoming increasingly evident: It's income that furnishes us with security, income that shapes our lifestyle choices. So why isn't there a greater focus on income planning? In my experience, when I meet with a prospective client and inquire about their plan, asking them to outline their income strategy and how all their financial pieces fit together, the response is often a concerning echo of uncertainty.

More often than not, they admit, "I'm here precisely because I don't have the answers to those questions." That admission is a crucial turning point. The time for action is now—this is why it's critical. You need a reliable income to secure your time and safeguard how you and your family live. Emphasizing the importance of a lifetime income stream is not just a financial strategy; it's a necessity that many overlook. Instead, we tend to rely on some heuristic we've heard about or place blind faith in our investment choices to deliver. However, the harsh truth is that these are mere estimates, rife with conjecture.

I know where I stand, and I've seen firsthand how my clients feel: They want clarity on their income sources and the assurance that it will endure. Does your current financial plan provide that certainty? Can it guarantee that you and your spouse will have a consistent income for life? If you're uncertain, it's time to consider an income plan. Such a plan can reveal any shortfalls or vulnerabilities in your financial strategy. Many have realized that Social Security alone won't suffice—they need to supplement it with personal savings.

The question then becomes: Do you prefer potential income or guaranteed income?

Reflect on your pension—if you're fortunate to have one—or imagine the security it could provide, akin to Social Security, offering a reliable stream of income monthly. That's powerful. I advocate for creating a lifetime income plan because I've witnessed its vital role in alleviating the anxiety of uncertain financial longevity. An income plan acts as your guide to a purposeful, well-timed, and enduring retirement. So, how do we construct this plan? Let's delve into that in the next chapter.

CHAPTER SIX

Buckets of Money

This book champions the idea that retirement offers the treasured opportunity to delve into your true calling. It's a time when your accumulated savings and assets take on a new role—supporting and enriching your life's purpose as much as possible within the bounds of thoughtful financial planning. You have a purpose in life, and the purpose of your money is to facilitate your engagement with what brings your life its most profound meaning while navigating the realities of your financial situation.

To make the most of your retirement savings, it's crucial to manage them wisely so they're ready to support your essential goals. But how do you do that effectively?

Many folks begin this journey on the wrong foot. They hunt for the "perfect" investment to grow their nest egg. Imagine I asked you, or pretty much anyone, to picture an ideal investment. Chances are, the list of features would look something like this:

- Safety – Nobody wants to gamble away their life's savings.
- Accessibility – It's essential to get to your money when life throws a curveball.
- Strong Growth – To combat inflation and ensure your funds last as long as you do.
- Tax Benefits – To safeguard your money from potential tax hikes down the road.
- Reliable Income for Life – Much like a pension, a steady cash flow you can rely on indefinitely.

A single investment that ticks all these boxes would be a dream come true. But the stark reality is that such an investment doesn't exist.

Every potential home for your money, from investments to savings accounts, carries its own set of pros and cons.

Luckily, there's a strategy to amplify the good points and mitigate the not-so-good, and it's all about segmenting your funds. This approach is a cornerstone of the guidance I offer my clients.

Retirement brings a mosaic of needs, goals, and time frames that should shape your investment decisions. By breaking up your resources—allocating portions to specific needs and the timing of those needs—you can more effectively match them with the right financial tools designed for each job.

Take liquidity, for instance. Life is full of surprises, and retirement is no exception. It's vital to earmark a slice of your assets for those just-in-case moments. Identifying this money's role makes it much simpler to pick out options that offer easy access—these are your go-to choices for liquid assets. Of course, they tend to lack in the growth department, but that's a compromise we accept. By limiting how much we set aside for liquidity—just enough to feel secure—we keep the larger portion of our portfolio free to chase other goals like growth, tax benefits, and more.

To bring the concept of this segmenting strategy to life, I often encourage my clients to picture their funds being split into separate "buckets." Each bucket correlates with a specific goal, fitting neatly into the broader picture of your investment approach and, by extension, your overarching financial plan. It's a straightforward method.

For clarity, let's consider just three buckets for now. I believe in demystifying financial concepts, making them easy to grasp and implement into your own financial planning.

Bucket #1 is what I like to call our Lifestyle Bucket—a term you might recall from an earlier discussion. This is the source of our retirement income; it's where our financial sustenance is stored. We also rely on

this bucket for an added layer of defense within our portfolio, and here's why that's crucial.

First, it's essential this bucket is insulated from any investment downturns. The goal is to safeguard what is arguably the most vital part of our financial well-being.

Second, this bucket's role in our broader financial strategy is to provide balance. Think of a traditional 40/60 split between stocks and bonds in a portfolio—the bonds are there to mitigate the volatility of stocks. However, we take it a step further within our Lifestyle Bucket by eliminating risk entirely. No exposure to the whims of bond markets here. And the reason? Simplicity itself. We'll be drawing on any funds allocated to this bucket regularly. We need absolute stability here to ensure you can live your life with peace of mind, free from the anxiety of market fluctuations impacting your essential income stream.

Our Lifestyle Bucket is intimately connected to a key figure—the monthly income we aspire to have in retirement. To shape this bucket effectively, we start by calculating "our number," which is the amount of money we envision needing each month to live comfortably and fulfill our dreams once we've retired. This number underpins our purpose and sets the benchmark for our desired lifestyle.

Then we tally up the guaranteed income we can already count on, like Social Security benefits or any pension income we're fortunate to have. With these figures in hand, we can pinpoint if there's a shortfall, an income gap that needs addressing. Filling this gap is essential, ensuring that our Lifestyle Bucket is not just a concept but a reliable financial resource that lets us enjoy our golden years to the fullest.

Let's consider a practical scenario involving a hypothetical married couple, Bill and Susan. Both aged sixty-two, and with retirement on the horizon, they have calculated they will need a monthly income of $6,500 to live the life they've envisioned once they stop working. This sum reflects their essential living costs and the extras for leisure and enjoyment. Their goal is to secure this amount as reliably as possible, ensuring they can savor their retirement without financial stress, emphasizing the paramount importance of safeguarding their lifestyle.

Upon reaching sixty-five, Bill is set to receive $2,800 in Social Security, with no pension to supplement this. Susan, also turning sixty-five, will get $1,450 from Social Security, again without a pension. Together, they'll have a monthly Social Security income of $4,250.

Year	Client Age	Spouse Age	Client Soc Sec	Spouse Soc Sec	Total Mo Gross Income	Annual Gross Income	Annual Gross Income Desired
1	65	65	$2,800	$1,450	$4,250	$51,000	$78,000

With their income goal of \$6,500 monthly (\$78,000 annually) and assuming a combined total of \$4,250 monthly (\$51,000 annually) coming from Social Security, they face a shortfall of \$2,250 each month (\$6,500 minus \$4,250 = \$2,250). This figure represents what they must draw from their savings to achieve their \$6,500 monthly lifestyle target.

Year	Client Age	Spouse Age	Client Soc Sec	Spouse Soc Sec	Total Mo Gross Income	Annual Gross Income	Annual Gross Income Desired
1	65	65	\$2,800	\$1,450	\$4,250	\$51,000	\$78,000
2	66	66	\$2,856	\$1,479	\$4,335	\$52,020	\$80,340
3	67	67	\$2,913	\$1,509	\$4,422	\$53,064	\$82,750
4	68	68	\$2,971	\$1,539	\$4,510	\$54,120	\$85,233
5	69	69	\$3,030	\$1,570	\$4,600	\$55,200	\$87,790
6	70	70	\$3,091	\$1,601	\$4,692	\$56,304	\$90,424
7	71	71	\$3,153	\$1,633	\$4,786	\$57,432	\$93,137
8	72	72	\$3,216	\$1,666	\$4,882	\$58,584	\$95,931
9	73	73	\$3,280	\$1,699	\$4,979	\$59,748	\$98,809
10	74	74	\$3,346	\$1,733	\$5,079	\$60,948	\$101,773
11	75	75	\$3,413	\$1,768	\$5,181	\$62,172	\$104,826
12	76	76	\$3,481	\$1,803	\$5,284	\$63,408	\$107,971
13	77	77	\$3,551	\$1,839	\$5,390	\$64,680	\$111,210
14	78	78	\$3,622	\$1,876	\$5,498	\$65,976	\$114,546
15	79	79	\$3,694	\$1,914	\$5,608	\$67,296	\$117,982
16	80	80	\$3,768	\$1,952	\$5,720	\$68,640	\$121,521
17	81	81	\$3,843	\$1,991	\$5,834	\$70,008	\$125,167
18	82	82	\$3,920	\$2,031	\$5,951	\$71,412	\$128,922
19	83	83	\$3,998	\$2,072	\$6,070	\$72,840	\$132,790
20	84	84	\$4,078	\$2,113	\$6,191	\$74,292	\$136,774
21	85	85	\$4,160	\$2,155	\$6,315	\$75,780	\$140,877
22	86	86	\$4,243	\$2,198	\$6,441	\$77,292	\$145,103
23	87	87	\$4,328	\$2,242	\$6,570	\$78,840	\$149,456
24	88	88	\$4,415	\$2,287	\$6,702	\$80,424	\$153,940
25	89	89	\$4,503	\$2,333	\$6,836	\$82,032	\$158,558

It should be noted that there are potentially many ways to optimize Social Security benefits depending on a person's specific circumstances. It's akin to a strategy game; mastering the nuances can significantly enhance your financial security during retirement. In my practice, I regularly work with clients to navigate these choices, tailoring strategies to fit each individual's financial plan and ensuring they maximize their benefits.

Inflation means the cost of living goes up over time. For Bill and Susan, this means they'll need more money each year to cover the same expenses. Even though their Social Security payments increase a little each year, it's not enough to keep up with how much faster prices are rising. This creates a gap between the money they have and the money they need.

As noted from the table above, upon reaching the age of seventy-five (in the eleventh year), their projected annual income from combined Social Security is $62,172, while the amount of desired income to meet expenses has grown to $104,826 due to the effects of inflation.

Year	Age	Retirement Balance	Retirement Fund Drawdowns	Total Income	Projected Expenses	Tax	Covered Expenses
2027	65	$680,400	$27,000	$51,000	$78,000	$0	$78,000

Fortunately, the couple has diligently built up a nest egg to help fill this gap. Their savings include a 401(k) with a balance of $450,000, thanks to their annual contributions of $15,000. Additionally, they have accumulated $150,000 in a brokerage account.

As Bill and Susan approached retirement, they decided to change their investment strategy to be more cautious. Initially, they mixed their investments between stocks (40 percent) for growth and bonds (60 percent) for stability. But when they retired, they moved all their money into bonds. This change was made to reduce the risk of losing money and ensure a more stable income from their investments.

They anticipate that these allocations will result in a 5 percent return on their investments before retirement, adjusting to a 4.5 percent return once they retire.

Remember, these returns are hypothetical and are used to demonstrate the impact of withdrawing from their savings to cover their retirement needs.

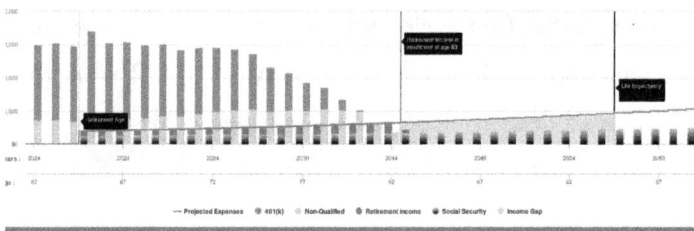

Referring to the graph above, the issue is that with ever-increasing drawdowns from their nest egg to meet the growing income gap, their savings begin to diminish rapidly. Based on the anticipated returns, hypothetical projections show that by the time both have reached the age of eighty-three, they will have drawn down both their 401(k) and brokerage account balances. From that point on, Bill and Susan's only remaining source of income would be from Social Security, leaving a significant gap between the income they had hoped for and what is actually available to sustain them later in life.

The major concern with depleting their nest egg by age eighty-three is that most Americans are living longer. On average, men who have reached age sixty-five can expect to live to about 84.1 years, while women who have reached age sixty-five can expect to live to about 86.8 years.[5]

How long will Bill and Susan live? If they knew the exact answer, planning for lifelong income would be much simpler. Instead, a solid retirement income plan must consider a variety of possible scenarios, aiming to strike a balance between maximizing annual income and ensuring they won't run out of money during their golden years.

It's surprisingly common for many new clients I meet to lack a solid income plan. Often, they're operating on a "maybe" plan—a scenario filled with uncertainty about how much income they'll receive and where it will come from. The urgency of addressing the question, "Why live in uncertainty?" cannot be overstated.

---

5   Social Security Administration. "Important Things to Consider When Planning for Retirement: What is Your Life Expectancy." https://www.ssa. gov/benefits/retirement/planner/otherthings.html?tl=1

Some Wall Street brokers might advise adopting a more aggressive investment strategy than the 100 percent allocation to bonds while in retirement as the only way to achieve the desired income while increasing the chances that the savings will last longer.

However, this suggestion is at odds with the insights shared in Chapter Four regarding the intrinsic link between risk and reward. Indeed, while more aggressive investment options may promise higher returns than the conservative bond portfolio chosen by Bill and Susan, they also carry a significantly higher risk of investment losses. Retirement is a phase of life where the stakes are too high for risky gambles with your life savings.

Recognizing the challenges is one thing, but solving them is another. While multiple approaches exist to manage this income gap, let's focus on establishing what I refer to as an "income bucket" to serve as a personal pension. The core purpose of this bucket is to safeguard what matters most—your reliable income stream, akin to the steady paycheck of your working years. It's paramount to understand where your income will come from and ensure it is dependable and sufficient. Your plan should always provide clear answers to these concerns, allowing you to live with peace of mind. To bridge the income gap, Bill and Susan should consider the use of a fixed indexed annuity. A primary reason is that fixed index annuities provide a standout feature: the ability to protect your capital from loss. This makes them an attractive option for those seeking to secure their income without the anxiety of potential market downturns.

While some Wall Street brokers might view my recommendation of using an annuity for the funds allocated to Bucket #1 as overly cautious, it's important to address a common misconception. Annuities, often misunderstood and sometimes presented as cure-alls for financial planning, actually serve a very specific purpose when used correctly. They are not a one-size-fits-all solution but are highly effective in certain scenarios, particularly in providing a steady income stream in retirement.

Bill and Susan, like many retirees, require a reliable source of income to secure a comfortable retirement. Most income sources, with the exception of annuities, fall short in one critical area—they don't provide income for life. To truly rest easy, retirees need the assurance that comes from knowing they have an income that won't run out, no matter how long they live. This is where the unique value of the right kind of annuity comes into play: it offers a check that arrives month after month for life.

Here lies a fundamental misunderstanding among many investment professionals. If a portion of a retiree's savings can be allocated to generate protected lifetime income, it opens up the opportunity to pursue potentially higher returns with the remainder of their portfolio without compromising their financial stability.

By choosing this path, Bill and Susan are able to enjoy the best of both worlds: the security of guaranteed income alongside the growth potential of their other investments. This strategic balance is the cornerstone of their retirement plan.

With this in mind, Bill and Susan decided to allocate a portion of their savings into a specific type of annuity known as an indexed annuity. By adding a lifetime income rider to this annuity it guarantees them a steady income for life, much like a regular paycheck, with the guarantee based on the claims-paying ability of the issuing insurance company. This rider comes with additional costs. Bill and Susan considered these extra costs worthwhile for the financial security and peace of mind the lifetime income provides.

After securing a reliable lifetime income with Bucket #1, Bill and Susan can shift their strategy for the funds in Buckets #2 and #3. Opting for a 60 percent stocks to 40 percent bonds allocation for Buckets #2 and #3 allows them to pursue growth potential while maintaining a measure of stability. This adjusted risk posture reflects their confidence in their foundational income and opens the door to potentially higher returns on their remaining assets.

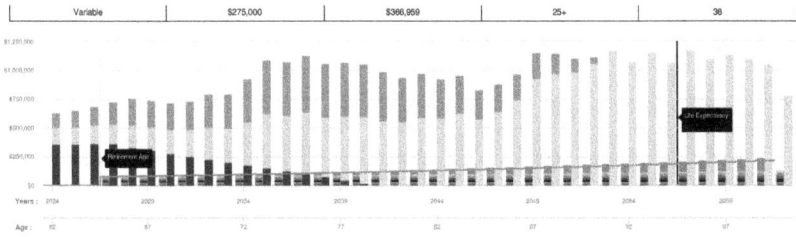

The decision to allocate $325,000 to this annuity was made because it is projected to provide sufficient additional lifetime income, which, along with their combined Social Security, would allow them to enjoy the income they desire throughout their retirement.

Annuities come in many varieties, with different insurance companies offering products that have unique features, benefits, and associated costs. The choice made by Bill and Susan serves as a mere example; what suits them may not be the best option for everyone. Carefully reviewing the specifics of each annuity and considering your own retirement needs is crucial. Providing guidance in evaluating these options to determine if an annuity fits your unique situation is a key part of how I assist my clients.

Bucket #2 is what I like to call your Contingency Bucket, but it might as well be named the "what if" bucket. It's crucial to understand that this isn't your emergency fund, which should be in cash or near-cash assets for immediate access.

The Contingency Bucket is there for the unforeseen, the variables that can nudge your monthly income and affect your lifestyle—things like rising costs due to inflation or unexpected healthcare expenses.

This bucket should align with your broader investment strategy, snugly fitting into your financial blueprint. Here, we lean towards investments with lower risk profiles, those that generate regular interest or dividends. We're aiming for a stable yield without overstepping into high-risk territory. While I won't dive into specific investment options here, the principle is to balance safety with some level of return in service of those potential extra costs that life might throw at you in retirement.

Consider another hypothetical example involving Joe and Jane, who have $600,000 in assets ready for retirement planning. They opted to transfer $275,000 into their first bucket—their solid foundation for income with zero investment loss risk. This strategic move leaves them with $325,000 for the second bucket, which is designated for their "future" income needs.

Here's where timing comes into play: The second bucket benefits from patience. By delaying the need to tap into this bucket, Joe and Jane can give their investments time to potentially grow. After careful consideration of their risk tolerance and future income requirements, they decided to allocate $150,000 to this second bucket.

Now, let's keep it simple for a moment. Imagine the $150,000 sits there, staying static to demonstrate the concept more clearly. If this bucket yielded a 3.0 percent return, that would generate $4,500 annually. A 3.5 percent return bumps the annual income to $5,250, and at 4 percent, we're looking at $6,000. This example isn't about the specifics of growth; it's to illustrate the process and the logic behind these strategic bucket allocations.

Imagine, three years into retirement, Joe and Jane notice their costs creeping up, subtly encroaching on the lifestyle they cherish. No need for alarm—their foresight in planning has provided a safety net. They now require a modest bump in their monthly budget—an additional $200 to maintain their standard of living.

Keeping to the conservative end of the spectrum, let's say their account has been yielding 3 percent. It's time to activate their "raise." From the $4,500 annual yield of their contingency bucket, they decide to withdraw $2,400, equivalent to their needed $200 per month increase. Post-withdrawal, they're left with $2,100 annually, which can be rolled over and reinvested to foster the bucket's growth.

This maneuver by Joe and Jane exemplifies the strategic brilliance of their plan—creating a flexible, responsive reservoir of funds tailored to address future financial needs. It ensures they can enjoy their golden years with peace of mind, knowing they've prepared not just for the present but for the evolving nature of retirement expenses. As this bucket continues to mature, its yield potential climbs, bolstering their ability to handle whatever life may throw their way without disrupting the integrity of the other carefully curated buckets in their retirement strategy.

Bucket #3 is akin to the long-range visionary of your financial arsenal, tagged as the Long-Term Growth Bucket. This is where you park your capital that won't be called upon for years, perhaps not until the later stages of your retirement. In this bucket, you can afford to ride the proverbial roller coaster of the stock market, enduring its dips and dives with the reassurance of time on your side.

The conventional wisdom espoused by Wall Street—urging investors to look past the short-term fluctuations and to remain steadfast with an eye on the distant horizon—fits well with this bucket's philosophy. However, this is not a one-size-fits-all strategy. The appropriateness of such an approach hinges critically on the timeline for when the funds will be required. It is prudent to avoid exposing the money set aside for near-term needs to significant volatility, as there isn't sufficient time to recover from potential market losses.

In stark contrast, this third bucket, earmarked for the future, can align with more aggressive investments such as stocks or stock funds. Here, you are afforded the luxury of patience, enabling you to weather the market's inevitable cycles of ebb and flow. By segregating your assets into these strategic buckets, you effectively insulate your short-term and medium-term financial needs from the inherent risks of long-term investing while still positioning yourself to capitalize on the growth potential offered by the stock market over time.

Striking the Right Balance in Bucket Strategy Planning

In the world of retirement planning, the concept of bucket strategy is both powerful and widely recognized. However, as with any approach, its success hinges on thoughtful execution and balance. The key lies in understanding what each bucket is designed to do and how much of your financial resources should be allocated to them.

One common pitfall in bucket strategy planning is the tendency to overfill one bucket due to its perceived benefits, often at the expense of others. For instance, if you pour too much into a bucket designed for income generation, such as an annuity, you might compromise the effectiveness of your other buckets. It's crucial to remember that retirement planning is a juggling act. Overcommitting to one aspect can throw off the balance, leaving other critical areas underfunded.

The age-old wisdom of not putting all your eggs in one basket rings especially true here. Diversification isn't just about spreading your investments across different asset classes; it's also about appropriately distributing your wealth across various strategies and purposes. Each bucket in your retirement plan serves a unique function—from ensuring immediate liquidity to fostering long-term growth. By overfilling one, you diminish your plan's overall flexibility and resilience.

Annuities can be an effective tool in retirement income planning, offering a steady income stream akin to a pension. However, they're not a one-size-fits-all solution. When I encounter new clients seeking a second opinion on their existing bucket plans, I often find an over-reliance on annuities, especially in the second bucket. While annuities have their place, a disproportionately large allocation raises questions. Is this the most suitable approach for the client's unique financial situation, or is it influenced more by the advisor's commission or a misunderstanding of the product's limitations?

As an advisor, my role is to ensure that each component of your retirement plan aligns with your specific needs and goals. This involves a careful examination of your financial situation and an honest assessment of the suitability of each investment. It's about putting your interests first and ensuring every recommendation enhances your plan's efficacy without undue risk or unnecessary costs.

The essence of successful bucket strategy planning lies in balance and personalization. Your retirement plan should be as unique as you are, reflecting your needs, goals, and circumstances. It's about finding the right mix, the perfect allocation that allows each bucket to fulfill its role effectively without overreliance on any single strategy. Remember, the best retirement plan provides not just financial security but peace of mind, and confidence that your assets are working in harmony to support the retirement you've envisioned.

CHAPTER SEVEN

Optimizing Social Security

So, how can you play it safe but still stay on course for the retirement you dream of? A big piece of the puzzle that many miss is getting smart about Social Security. We've all heard bits and pieces about it, right? But why is it a big deal? Well, how you decide to take Social Security can impact your financial plan and your life.

In my experience, many people start taking their Social Security as soon as they retire. It makes sense on the surface—they need the money since their regular paycheck has stopped. Whether they retire at sixty-two, sixty-five, sixty-six, or another age, they often think, "I've got this benefit, might as well use it." But here's where we might stumble. Did we stop to think if it's the best move, or are we just going with what we know?

Your approach to Social Security should be as unique as you are—it's not something you copy from a friend or family member. It's got to suit your needs. If you wait to take Social Security, what happens to your savings? What about taxes? And if you take it too early, will it reduce what your spouse gets after you're gone? These are the kinds of things you need to think through because getting it right means you can get more without taking more risks.

Social Security offers a reliable and consistent income stream for life, ideally positioning it as a critical element of Bucket #1 in your financial blueprint. The more substantial your Social Security benefit, the less you need to rely on your savings to bridge any income gaps in your retirement plan. Consequently, you can allocate more of your savings to the second and third buckets, potentially fortifying your financial foundation.

To optimize your Social Security payout, it's essential to understand your choices regarding the commencement of your benefits. There's a wide range of options, especially for married couples, with the potential for thousands of start-date combinations to consider. This breadth of choice underscores the need for a tailored approach to selecting the optimal time to activate your Social Security income stream.

The timing of when you decide to initiate your retirement benefit or your spousal benefit will set the stage for the monthly amount you'll receive indefinitely. And it isn't just a matter of what year you choose to start; the specific month within that year that you elect to begin your benefits can significantly affect your payment amount. Each month matters in calculating your lifelong income from Social Security.

The amount of money you get from Social Security depends on your past earnings and when you choose to start taking your benefits. Suppose someone born in 1952 could get $1,000 a month if they start at sixty-two, the youngest age to begin. If they wait longer to take the benefit, the monthly amount goes up. Here's a table to show how much that $1,000 increases each year they delay starting their benefits.

Benefit Start Age	Monthly Income
62	$1,000
63	$1,066
64	$1,155
65	$1,245
66	$1,333
67	$1,440
68	$1,546
69	$1,653
70	$1,760

Social Security allows you to start receiving benefits at any time from age sixty-two up to age seventy, and you can choose to begin in any month during that range. A more accurate version of the above chart would show the exact benefit amounts if this person started their benefit at age sixty-six, sixty-six and one month, sixty-six and two months, and so on. The main point is the later you choose to start your benefits, the more you'll receive each month.

You've paid into Social Security with your payroll taxes throughout your career. Unlike a personal investment account that grows over time, this money isn't stored in a personal fund just for you. However, it's interesting to think about what size investment you'd need to match the income Social Security provides.

Let's say an investment could give you a yearly income of 5 percent of its value. The table below would then show you how much you need in that investment to equal the monthly Social Security income mentioned earlier.

Benefit Start Age	Monthly Income	Balance Required*
62	$1,000	$239,940
63	$1,066	$255,936
64	$1,155	$277,243
65	$1,245	$298,581
66	$1,333	$319,920

Benefit Start Age	Monthly Income	Balance Required*
67	$1,440	$345,514
68	$1,546	$371,107
69	$1,653	$396,701
70	$1,760	$422,294

Assuming 5 percent cash flow

Consider it like this: Without Social Security, you'd need to have saved up $239,940 by the time you're sixty-two to get a monthly income of $1,000 if your investments pay out 5 percent per year. If you wait until you're seventy, you'd need a nest egg of $422,284 to receive $1,760 each month, again based on a 5 percent payout.

The difference between starting Social Security at sixty-two and waiting until seventy—that extra $760 monthly (going from $1,000 to $1,760)—is comparable to having an additional $182,354 ($422,294 minus $239,940) invested.

Put another way, if you find yourself short on savings as you approach retirement, one strategy to boost your financial security is to postpone taking Social Security. This delay increases your monthly benefit, acting like a bolster to your income without needing the equivalent savings in the bank.

It's true; some may critique this viewpoint by mentioning that if you begin collecting Social Security early and invest those payments, you could potentially grow another pot of money for later in retirement.

This perspective has merit and is why some retirees opt to take Social Security earlier, even when they don't immediately need the funds.

Deciding whether to take a smaller Social Security payment earlier or a larger one later hinges on various factors. These include your life expectancy, the anticipated return on your investments, projected inflation rates, and expected tax obligations. The best approach for one person may not be the same for another, as it all boils down to individual circumstances.

Benefits for Widows and Widowers Regarding Social Security

Cost-of-Living Adjustments (COLAs) and delayed retirement credits can significantly affect widows and widowers. To grasp the extent of this impact, it's crucial to distinguish how delayed retirement credits influence spousal benefits, which often leads to confusion. An example can provide clarity.

Consider Mark and Maria, both sixty-two years old and married. Mark has a more substantial work and earnings record with Social Security, as Maria took time off work to raise their children. As a result, her spousal benefit from Social Security will be greater than the benefit she would receive based on her work history, no matter when they start claiming benefits.

If Mark and Maria begin their benefits before reaching their full retirement age, both Mark's worker's benefit and Maria's spousal benefit would be permanently reduced. Should Mark postpone his worker's benefit past the full retirement age, he would gain an 8 percent annual increase, plus any COLAs for each year he delays up until age seventy. However, Maria's spousal benefit is not increased by delayed retirement credits. It is calculated as 50 percent of Mark's benefit as if he had started receiving it at full retirement age, not 50 percent of what his benefit would be had he waited until age seventy.

There's a common misunderstanding that delayed retirement credits (DRCs) do not boost the widow's benefit a surviving spouse would receive, but this is incorrect. While both are alive, spousal benefits provide either one's own worker's benefit or 50 percent of the other's as the spousal benefit. When one spouse passes away, the dynamic changes, allowing the surviving spouse to receive the larger of their own worker's benefit (including any COLAs) or 100 percent of the deceased spouse's benefit (including COLAs and DRCs).

This scenario dramatically benefits couples concerned about the financial well-being of the surviving spouse in the long term.

Tax Benefits of Social Security

The potential tax benefits embedded in Social Security are among its most advantageous features. In the upcoming chapter, we'll explore how, under the current tax laws, no more than 85 percent of your Social Security benefits may be subject to taxation. However, it's often possible to decrease this amount with strategic planning. If and when this can be accomplished, you increase a tax-free stream of income potentially for life.

In the next chapter, we'll delve deeper into the taxation of Social Security benefits, examine the broader implications of taxes on your retirement, and explore strategies to help you manage your tax obligations more effectively.

CHAPTER EIGHT

Tax Planning
Please Don't Feed the Beast

*"A taxpayer is someone who works for the federal
government but doesn't have to take a civil service
examination."* - **Ronald Reagan**

---

*Bill and Mary had been planning for their retirement
since they were in their early fifties. They looked forward
to the day when work was no longer a necessary part of
their lives, and they could finally have the time to do all
of the things that they wanted to do.*

*They knew they would need money to make their
retirement dreams come true, so they meticulously
planned out every detail of what their life would look
like after they stopped working. They budgeted all of*

the expenses they felt they would face— food, housing, insurance, and even accounting for the travel costs and other fun things they wanted to do.

But after retiring, they were shocked by the amount of one expense that had completely taken them by surprise—taxes! Once Bill and Mary realized how much of their savings would be going to taxes each year, it forced significant adjustments in their plans. After working so hard for so many years and thinking it was finally time to relax and enjoy themselves, it seemed a cruel joke that taxes turned out to have a sizable impact on the lifestyle they could enjoy in retirement.

People are shocked when they find that one of their biggest expenses in retirement can be taxes. It happens because so many people expect their taxes to lower once they stop working. The logic is that income will be less in retirement, so taxes will be less as well. But a few realities can easily turn this into a myth.

Many retirees face fewer tax breaks. For instance, they can't count on the mortgage interest deduction to lower their taxes after paying off their home loan. And with children grown and out of the house, those tax deductions disappear, too. This can make tax time tougher, especially if stopping work doesn't reduce their taxable income as much as they thought it would.

Many folks dream of traveling or picking up new hobbies in retirement, activities that can mean spending more money. If they pull this money from taxable accounts such as 401(k)s and IRAs, they could end up with a higher taxable income.

Even sadder is that taxes might be better managed with some proper planning. Don't make the mistake many people make when they allow themselves to be surprised by taxes unique to retirement.

Bracing for Higher Taxes: Navigating the Sunset of the Tax Cuts and Jobs Act in Retirement

As you approach retirement, a crucial factor shouldn't be overlooked: the potential for higher taxes. A significant reason for this is the scheduled expiration of the 2017 Tax Cuts and Jobs Act. When these tax cuts sunset in 2026, several favorable provisions that may have lowered your tax bill are set to reverse. Understanding this change is critical to ensuring you don't get an unwelcome surprise in your golden years.

First, the individual tax rates that were reduced by the 2017 law are set to increase again. This means that the income you draw from retirement accounts could be taxed at a higher rate than it is today. For many retirees, this could translate into a larger portion of their retirement savings going to Uncle Sam rather than funding their leisure years.

Moreover, the standard deduction, which was nearly doubled by the tax overhaul, will revert to its previous lower levels, adjusted for inflation. This reduction means that if you're not itemizing deductions, you'll have a smaller buffer to shield your income from taxes. For retirees counting on every dollar of their nest egg, this could mean the difference between a comfortable retirement and a financially strained one.

Additionally, the act's favorable rules for itemized deductions, including the expanded Child Tax Credit and the increased exemption for Alternative Minimum Tax (AMT), are set to roll back. These changes could lead to a higher effective tax rate, particularly for those who find themselves no longer shielded from the AMT—a tax mechanism that was designed to ensure that high-income earners pay a fair share of taxes.

US National Debt: Peering Into the Fiscal Abyss

If you're holding onto hope that Congress will swoop in and renew the tax reliefs introduced in the 2017 reforms, you're not alone. It's a thought that many cling to, especially when faced with the prospect of increased taxes. But as you plan your retirement, there are several points it might be wise to ponder.

As we recover from the economic upheaval caused by the COVID-19 pandemic, it's important to reflect on the financial responses that were deployed to mitigate its effects. The government issued three waves of stimulus payments to cushion the blow, targeting around 90 percent of taxpayers. Numerous households and businesses received significant sums, with some families receiving upwards of $10,000 in relief over the span of a year.

While these measures may have been necessary for staving off economic disaster, they also contributed to a soaring federal deficit. As we look to the future, this financial reality sets the stage for potential tax increases.

Indeed, the government didn't have a spare couple of trillion dollars waiting to be used, so how did they fund the massive stimulus packages? You've probably guessed it right. The government created the money, leading to a massive wave of new cash introduced into our economy, money that wasn't there before 2020.

To give you a perspective on the numbers, in February 2022, the US national debt tipped over the $30 trillion mark. And as of the latest update, it has climbed even higher to more than $33.7 trillion.

If you're braced for a bit of a jolt, take a moment to check out the website usdebtclock.org, which offers a real-time tally of the US national debt's relentless climb. By the time you're reading this, it wouldn't surprise me if that figure has soared past the $34 trillion mark—or even higher.

But perhaps what's more disheartening is the breakdown of this total debt when it's divided by the number of taxpayers in the country. At present, the debt owed for each taxpayer is beyond $250,000—a figure that's nothing short of astonishing.

These numbers are a wake-up call—they hint at a trend that's unsustainable in the long run. It's likely only a matter of time before tax rates climb, a change that could send ripples through many retirement plans. This is a stark reminder of why it's so critical for individuals to take proactive measures now to safeguard their future finances from these looming fiscal challenges.

Bracing for the Tax Tempest in Retirement

Did you ever think the tricky taxes you dealt with during your career were just a warm-up? You heard that right! Consider all the different places you've put your money for the golden years: your IRAs, your 401(k)s, the shares accumulating in your investment account, and let's not forget Social Security. These aren't just streams of cash; they're like unique pieces of a big tax puzzle. And here's something to ponder: Mixing and matching withdrawals from these pools can land you in a whole new world of tax outcomes. Some ways are smooth sailing—you keep more of your cash and pay the taxman less.

But take a different turn, and you might get a "thank-you!" from Uncle Sam for a hefty tax bill. We will unpack all this in this chapter. Every penny you fork over in taxes is one less penny for living out those retirement dreams.

Social Security Taxation

For those fresh to retirement's freedom, here's something that might startle you: your Social Security benefits could become a part of your tax bill! It's true not everyone is affected, but according to the folks handling our Social Security, more than half of recipients, 56 percent to be exact, are paying taxes on those benefits. And get this: up to 85 percent of your Social Security might be up for grabs by Uncle Sam.

Let's break it down: say you're on your own, raking in $50,000 yearly, with Social Security chipping in $1,500 monthly. That tallies up to $18,000 from Social Security per annum. But depending on the source of the $50,000, you might find up to $15,300 of your Social Security will be considered as additional taxable income. Take a moment and let that soak in.

The million-dollar question is, where's that $50,000 of income coming from? If it's withdrawals from a traditional IRA or 401(k), you might want to brace for a tax hit on your Social Security. But if that cash flow comes from, say, a Roth IRA, then you might just dance around the tax man.

I'm not here to tell you to rush out and flip your nest egg into a Roth. That could backfire for some. I am stressing the big part your income sources play in how much you'll owe the tax office.

Retirement Savings: The Tax Time Bomb in Your IRA and 401(k)

Let's shift gears to discuss your IRA, 401(k), and other similar retirement pots. These are the heavyweights of the retirement saving world. And the main draw? That tempting tax break you get right out the gate every time you add to the pot. It's an alluring benefit, seducing you with a tax break right here, right now.

But let's get something straight: These accounts aren't a tax-free haven. When it's time to tap into them, don't be caught off guard when a certain someone shows up, hand outstretched, for a piece of the pie. That's right, good old Uncle Sam. It's a detail that slips many minds, often left out of the retirement planning equation.

Here's a little thought experiment for the next time you review your retirement account statements. Envision it as a shared account, with Uncle Sam as your silent partner. And here's the twist: Trying to guess what Uncle Sam's share will be in the future is like trying to read tea leaves. Tax rates? Those are in the hands of Congress, and they've been known to shuffle those figures around. And let's not forget we're on a collision course with a tax rate increase come 2026.

So, what's the game plan? Can you outmaneuver this? Honestly, it's tough to say without knowing your specific situation. But one thing's crystal clear: now is the time to start looking at your options, to get ahead of the game and prep for when those tax rates take their inevitable leap.

Balancing Work Income and Retirement Benefits: A Taxing Puzzle

Now, let's delve into the often-overlooked tax conundrums that arise when you mix income from a part-time or full-time job with retirement. You might think, "Aren't taxes on employment income cut and dried?" Not so fast—throw retirement and Social Security into the mix, and things start to wrinkle.

Picture yourself not fully retired yet, drawing a paycheck that exceeds $21,240 for 2023. This is where the tax waters get murky. Earning a wage while collecting Social Security introduces a twist. It's not an outright tax, but it might pinch your pocket just as hard, if not harder. If your earnings are above that threshold, you'll find your Social Security benefits starting to shrink. For every $2 over the limit, the Social Security Administration will trim $1 from your benefits. This scaling back lessens and eventually stops once you hit full retirement age, but until you reach that milestone, it acts as a stealthy financial snare that can catch many off guard.

Roth IRAs: The Tax-Free Champion with a Catch

Let's spotlight Roth IRAs for a moment—the virtuoso of tax efficiency in retirement planning. Picture the Roth IRA as the superhero of the tax-saving world, donning a cape emblazoned with the phrase "tax-free." This is the battle cry of the Roth: Pull your money out and pay nothing to Uncle Sam. It won't even nudge the tax needle on your Social Security benefits. Sounds like a dream, doesn't it? But, as with every tale of heroism, there's a twist. Every superhero has a vulnerability, and the Roth IRA's kryptonite comes in the form of "qualified distributions." To ensure your withdrawals maintain their tax-free superpower, they must meet the IRS's standards. Slip up, and suddenly you're facing taxes and penalties—a potentially costly mistake that could dismantle your meticulously laid plans.

In essence, while Roth IRAs are indeed a potent tool in dodging taxes, they require careful navigation. Work with a financial advisor savvy in IRS regulations to ensure your Roth IRA maintains its heroic status, safeguarding you from any tax-time bombshells.

Other Income Sources: Navigating the Tax Maze

Diving into the tax intricacies of retirement may feel like entering a labyrinth, but it's worth exploring every avenue, including some of the roads less traveled. So, let's shine a light on other income sources that may not be as ubiquitous but are just as important to consider for their tax impact.

Pensions are the old guard of retirement income and come with a pivotal tax-related decision: should you go for the steady stream of lifetime income or take the lump sum offer? Both options have their own tax landscapes to navigate, and understanding the pros and cons is crucial for choosing the path that leads to tax efficiency.

Retirees need to be strategic regarding capital gains, especially if they hold investments outside the familiar confines of IRAs and the like. Knowing when to hold onto assets and when to let them go can play a significant role in managing your tax bill, thanks to the preferential treatment of long-term capital gains. And don't forget the considerable advantage of the step-up in basis, which can be a game-changer for estate planning.

Dividends are a welcome addition to any retiree's income stream, especially when they're qualified and eligible for lower tax rates. This can lead to a more tax-friendly approach to drawing income from your investment portfolio.

Lastly, there's the often-overlooked municipal bond. While it may sound like a small-town player, it can pack a tax-free punch at the federal level. But a word to the wise: Keep an eye on state taxes if those bonds hail from outside your home state.

Strategic Tax Planning

As we conclude this chapter, let's address a topic that often stirs up much public discourse: the perception that the affluent pay less than their "fair share" of taxes. Understandably, this can raise eyebrows, but let's peel back the curtain on what's really happening. It's not about the wealthy dodging taxes; instead, it's about how they navigate the complexities of the tax code crafted by lawmakers.

It's clear there are wide-ranging tax treatments for different streams of income, which opens the door to managing tax liabilities through savvy planning. Here's the twist: this isn't a strategy reserved for the top tier alone.

The unfortunate reality is that many people don't fully leverage long-term tax planning. For most, tax time is a once-a-year event where they submit their financials to a preparer and hope for the best. Yet, the well-informed and astute retirees understand this: Genuine tax planning is not about a yearly reaction to your tax bill. It's a forward-looking, strategic process. It's about aligning your assets and income in a way that smartly navigates the tax landscape of the future.

This approach is proactive, akin to a strategic game of chess where you plan several moves ahead.

Remember, the path to a rewarding retirement isn't solely about the amount you save or the yields of your investments. It's equally about employing the knowledge, foresight, and strategies that enable you to keep a greater share of your hard-earned wealth. It's about ensuring that every dollar you save works just as hard for you as you did for it.

CHAPTER NINE

Building Resilience into Your Retirement Plan

In the dance of life, it's the unexpected steps that often catch us off guard. As a seasoned financial advisor, I've seen that despite our best-laid plans, life has a way of throwing a wrench into the works. I can say with confidence, built on years of experience, that the unpredictable is a constant companion on our journey toward retirement.

When it comes to retirement planning, complexity is a given. There's a delicate interplay of variables and uncertainties that must be navigated with care. It's tempting to dwell on the present and base decisions on the current state of affairs. However, it's the forward-looking gaze—the one that scans the horizon for potential storms—that's critical for ensuring long-term financial well-being.

The cornerstone of preparing for life's surprises lies in crafting a robust retirement income plan. This isn't just any document; it's a written strategy that casts its projections into the future, grappling with assumptions about expenses, the relentless march of inflation, the growth trajectory of your savings, and the ever-evolving tax landscape. It's your financial forecast, designed to unveil risks and equip you with strategies for the unforeseen.

Having etched your plan in ink, it's vital not to let it gather dust. An annual ritual should be to put your plan under the microscope—reviewing, refining, and recalibrating based on the shifting sands of your life and the world around you. This is not a mere check-in; it's a strategic overhaul to ensure life's twists and turns don't derail your retirement goals.

Let's consider the myriad forms of these unexpected events: a health crisis that leaps out of the shadows, an economic tempest that shakes the markets, or a natural calamity that upends communities. A robust retirement income plan is your financial bulwark against these tides of fate.

The emergency fund is another critical aspect often overlooked—a financial shock absorber. This is your safeguard, the reserve that stands between you and the need to encroach upon your retirement nest egg when life hits you with unforeseen expenses. The rule of thumb—keeping aside three to six months' worth of expenses—can be a lifeline when the seas get rough.

Bracing for life's surprises is an indispensable facet of retirement planning. A well-conceived, dynamic retirement income plan, coupled with a solid emergency fund, serves as your financial armor against the vagaries of the future, safeguarding the fruits of your lifelong labor.

Now, let's explore a common scenario. Often, individuals walk into my office brandishing a folder—the kind that crinkles with the weight of statements. They lay it out like a deck of cards, each one a snapshot of their savings. When I probe deeper, asking about their plan, they point to the same stack. But those are merely statements, a record of transactions, not a strategy.

This is where I introduce them to the litmus test of financial planning. A sound plan should have answers, or at least contingencies, for the following: What if the markets plunge? What if the economy staggers into a decade-long lull? What if inflation rears its head or interest rates plummet? What if health becomes a hurdle, or if the unthinkable happens, and a partner passes away? If the response to these is a furrowed brow, they possess a collection of statements, not a plan.

A genuine financial strategy is not just about the allocation of assets. It's a detailed blueprint that uses investments as tools to build a resilient structure. It's about having a plan that ensures, come what may, your retirement vision remains unclouded.

What does this mean for you? It means confidence—the kind that comes from knowing you've anticipated and planned for the "what ifs." It provides peace of mind, allowing you to live your life liberated from the shackles of financial worry. This is the true essence of a financial plan: not just to survive the storms but to navigate through them with assurance, knowing that your course is true, your preparations thorough, and your future secure.

Thus, as we chart this complex journey, remember that a retirement plan is more than a static document—it's an evolving strategy that adapts to life's ever-changing narrative. It's about taking control, staying vigilant, and moving forward with the certainty that you are as prepared as one can be for whatever lies ahead. It's about making sure that when the unexpected comes knocking, you can answer with a smile, knowing you've got everything in place.

The Perils of Procrastination

There's another crucial aspect of retirement planning that often goes overlooked: the danger of procrastination.

Procrastination in retirement planning can be a subtle yet destructive force, and to illustrate its impact, I'd like to share the story of a client named Jeff. Jeff's dream was simple yet profound: to travel and explore the United States in his retirement years. He envisioned a life on the road, discovering the diverse landscapes and cultures stitching this vast country's fabric. But there was a hitch—Jeff was caught in the trap of chasing an elusive financial target before he could start his journey.

Jeff had absorbed the common notion that one must accumulate a specific, almost magical amount of savings before embracing retirement. This belief led him to delay his dream continually, always waiting for the right financial moment. However, life, as it often does, threw a wrench into his plans. What started as minor health issues cascaded into a series of debilitating problems. By the time Jeff reached his financial goal, his physical condition no longer allowed him the freedom to travel. Long car rides or flights became impossible, and his ability to walk and stand for extended periods was severely limited.

When Jeff first became my client, his priorities had shifted drastically. The man who once dreamed of national parks and road trips now faced a reality where his focus was on health and accessibility. His financial resources, once earmarked for adventure, were now redirected towards modifying his home for better accessibility and preparing for the future well-being of his wife. Jeff confided in me, expressing regret and surprise at how his circumstances had evolved so unpredictably.

This story of Jeff isn't just a tale of unfulfilled dreams; it's a cautionary lesson about the risks of postponing retirement planning. Had Jeff sought financial guidance earlier, we could have addressed these issues proactively. Our planning would have included strategies for health-related contingencies and survivorship planning, ensuring a smoother transition through life's unpredictable twists and turns.

Jeff's experience underlines a fundamental truth in retirement planning: Time is as much a currency as money itself. The earlier you start planning, the more options you have, and the better prepared you are to adapt to life's surprises. Procrastination can cost more than just time; it can cost dreams.

In our work together, Jeff and I focused on making the best of his current situation, ensuring his and his wife's comfort and security. But he often expressed one regret: "I wish I had started sooner."

So let Jeff's story be a reminder: Don't wait for a perfect financial number to start living your retirement dream. Consult with a financial advisor, assess your current situation, and start planning. You might discover that your dream retirement is more achievable than you think, or you might need to adapt your plan to new realities. Either way, taking action now can make a significant difference.

Your retirement plan should be a living document that evolves with your life's journey. It's not just about safeguarding your finances; it's about enabling you to live your life to the fullest, regardless of what the future holds. Start now and pave the way for a resilient, fulfilling retirement that aligns with your dreams and values.

CHAPTER TEN

Your Fourth Bucket:

Finding Fulfillment Beyond Finances

"A person really doesn't become whole, until he becomes a part of something that's bigger than himself." - Jim Valvano

In Chapter Six, we delved deep into the strategy of using three buckets to allocate retirement savings, each tailored to specific financial needs and objectives. This approach forms a robust framework for achieving a secure and well-planned retirement. However, my three decades as a financial advisor have taught me an invaluable lesson: financial stability, while crucial, doesn't automatically translate into a fulfilling retirement.

It's not uncommon to encounter individuals who, despite having ample financial resources, grapple with a sense of dissatisfaction in their retirement years. This unhappiness often stems from non-financial factors like boredom, a lost sense of purpose, or the struggle to find meaningful engagement.

A recurring pattern in my career has been observing that the most contented retirees are those who invest their time and resources in serving and uplifting others. They've discovered a profound truth: A life dedicated to contributing positively to the world around them is a life brimming with purpose and joy.

Initially, my focus as a financial advisor was predominantly on the monetary aspects of retirement planning. It seemed straightforward—ensure long-term financial security for my clients, and my job was done. However, as I matured in my profession, I gained a broader perspective. To truly assist my clients in achieving a richly rewarding retirement, guiding them in creating a life that extends beyond financial comfort is imperative. This means encouraging avenues for meaningful contribution and service.

There are essentially two paths to making such a contribution. The first involves financial support for charities, causes, and community projects. The US tax code, fortunately, is replete with incentives for charitable giving. Over the years, I've honed my skills in optimizing the impact of my clients' financial contributions to their chosen causes.

Yet, monetary donations may not resonate as deeply with everyone. There's an incomparable value in volunteering time and energy. When we offer our time, we engage more personally, fostering connections that bring a different dimension of fulfillment and joy.

This brings us to a crucial realization: In retirement, "time" becomes an invaluable asset, possibly surpassing the value of monetary resources. The older we get, the more precious each moment becomes.

Herein lies the intriguing link between our financial and temporal assets. Our savings bankroll our retirement activities, while retirement bestows upon us the gift of time. It's this time that can be channeled into pursuits that enrich not just our lives but the lives of others as well.

Thus, I propose the concept of a Fourth Bucket. This isn't about financial planning; it's about planning for the time you now possess. What do you plan to do with the hours, days, and years that retirement affords you? The Fourth Bucket is a call to action, nudging you to utilize your time in meaningful ways. It could be volunteering, mentoring, participating in community service, or any form of giving back that aligns with your passions and skills.

In essence, the Fourth Bucket isn't about financial assets; it's about leveraging your time, talents, and experience for the greater good. It's about filling the void that financial success alone cannot address. It's about realizing your potential in ways that bring a sense of achievement and purpose. As the saying goes, "God's greatest gift to us is potential. Our greatest gift to God is to realize it." Let this Fourth Bucket be your guide to a retirement life rich in purpose and fulfillment.

CHAPTER ELEVEN

Create the Retirement Life You Want

Why shouldn't we be happier when we retire? What stands in the way is that, for some reason, we define retirement by spending money. Because of this mantra, we worry. We worry about whether or not things are really going to work out. What should we be doing? We should be finding our purpose first and foremost. Successful retirements are not based on how much money we spend, but that is our definition for some reason.

Bestselling financial author David Bach put it best when I heard him speak once about material possessions some desire while admitting "life is too short," to justify a big purchase. David mentioned the Corvette someone always wanted, or a bigger house. Then he went on to wonder why it is some overlook personal betterment. Rather than spend more money, he reasoned, why not spend more time on activities such as reading, exercising, and gardening?

Or, most importantly, how about spending more time with family?

Do you get my point? Spending money without a purpose is not going to make you happier. Buying the Corvette might initially, but it's material. Life is about living and enjoying the simple things: Waking up in the morning and watching the sunrise, the smell of spring, tasting good food, and spending time with those we love. That is living. What do you love, or who you love?

So often, when I ask a new client what it is they want, I get a blank stare. When we focus on what we want, we find our purpose. Your purpose will drive your goals; it will drive your lifestyle. It will dictate the how and what you do and how you do it. Keep in mind it wasn't or isn't necessarily the job that you hate. It's the commitment of the job that bothers you. You HAVE to be somewhere. It takes up your time. It's the same routine day in and day out. It's the time constraint that bothers us the most if we dig deep inside of ourselves. It's that constant need to be somewhere. It interferes with things that we want to do. We yearn for the things we love and want to do, but that job keeps getting in the way. Right?

The problem is that we do not give ourselves enough time to think about how great it would be not to have that commitment. Do not take time for granted. Time is the basis by which we live our lives. From hours in a day and night, to weeks, to months to years. It defines us. Now, sit back and imagine what you would do if you had all the time in the world. What would you do?

I guarantee that once you stop to think about it, it isn't ALWAYS about spending money. Consider spending more time with your family, exercising more, starting the hobby you love but don't have the time for, and doing more for servitude by dedicating more time to helping others. This is fulfillment. It still gives us a sense of accomplishment. It is actionable, and it can be measured.

These are also things that help us engage our mind, body, and spirit. It makes us happy and fulfilled. This is finding your purpose. This is what should drive you day in and day out. Spending my life worrying about money, the markets, whether I have done enough, my health, and my job causes so much stress and doesn't allow us to smile.

The key is taking the worry out of these things so you can live a happy, long life. It's about defining your purpose and building your plan around. Please do not get me wrong, I don't mean that you shouldn't spend your money on material things, vacations, etc. I am simply saying do not let that be the complete driver to happiness.

If I build my plan around the time I am here on earth, the blessed time that I am given by not having the commitment of my job, then I can focus on what will make me happy. Happy, healthy people live longer lives. Make sure your income plan allows you the freedom to enjoy your life without worry so that you can be happy, healthy, and here for a long time.

About the Author

CHRISTOPHER MEDIATE, MBA, CWM, RFC
President, Mediate Financial Services

Christopher Mediate stands at the forefront of retirement planning, dedicating over a quarter-century to guiding retirees and baby boomers towards a secure and fulfilling retirement. His expertise and strategic approach have positioned him as a trusted advisor in the complex realm of financial security and wealth management.

A Youngstown, Ohio native, Chris's academic journey culminated with an MBA from Webster University, laying the groundwork for his distinguished career as a financial advisor. In 1994, he founded Mediate Financial Investment Advisory Services, LLC, with a mission to offer bespoke retirement strategies that address the unique challenges and goals of each client. Chris's credentials include Chartered Wealth Manager, Registered Financial Consultant, Series 65 securities exam completion, and comprehensive insurance licensure. His role as an Investment Adviser Representative binds him to a fiduciary standard, ensuring client interests are paramount.

Chris's contributions to the field extend beyond individual client consultations. He is a recognized speaker on tax planning in retirement, earning accolades such as the Ambassador Award from Public Employee Retirees, Inc., for his dedication to educating the public on financial wellness in retirement.

His personal commitment to preparedness and resilience was put to the test following a life-altering injury in 2013. The experience deepened his resolve to equip others with the knowledge and tools to navigate life's uncertainties with confidence.

Today, Chris leverages his profound understanding of financial instruments and investment strategies to empower individuals to optimize their retirement planning. He hosts the educational program "Retirement in Focus" on WFMJ and WKBN, further extending his reach and impact.

Residing in Youngstown with his wife Leslie and their two sons, Chris has woven his family values into the fabric of his business, creating a firm that epitomizes trust, integrity, and a personalized touch in retirement planning.

Discover more about Chris's approach to retirement planning at MediateFinancial.com, where insight meets action to forge pathways to a secure retirement.

www.ingramcontent.com/pod-product-compliance
Lightning Source LLC
Chambersburg PA
CBHW022043210326
41458CB00087B/6875/J